BURNED OUT

CHELAN COUNTY FIRES 2015

COVER PHOTO SUBMITTED BY GRACE WATKINS
VIEW FROM MANSON, WA
FIRST CREEK FIRE

BACK COVER PHOTO SUBMITTED BY NANCY CULP
VIEW FROM LAKE CHELAN, WA
HER FAMILY CABINS BURN

COMPILED BY C. MARCHI

MOVING FORWARD

*THIS BOOK WAS COMPILED FROM PARTICIPATING RESIDENTS OF
LAKE CHELAN, WA.
THE CHELAN REBEL WRITERS GROUP SUGGESTED MAKING
AVAILABLE TO OUR COMMUNITY A METHOD IN WHICH TO HEAL
THROUGH THE ART OF SCRIBE.*

*THESE STORIES, POEMS AND THOUGHTS WERE WRITTEN IN THE
AUTHORS' OWN WORDS, EXPRESSING THE STRESS OF BEING
SURROUNDED BY INTENSE FIRES AND THE UNKNOWN OUTCOME.
EDITED FIRE AND RESCUE LOGS ARE INCLUDED.*

*PROCEEDS RETURN TO THOSE AFFECTED BY THIS UNFORTUNATE
EVENT. YOUR CONTRIBUTIONS ARE GREATLY APPRECIATED.*

Contents

DROUGHT

Conditions presented themselves in 2014 and 2015. An estimated 1.2 million homes across 13 western states were at high or very high risk of wildfires. June 28 2015, Sleepy Hollow Fire burned 3,000 acres and burned Wenatchee, WA homes, including a number of industrial buildings all within a 24-hour period.

Uplake in Lake Chelan, WA, the Wolverine Fire near Lucerne/Holden Village started in June 2015.

August 14, 2015 a dry lightning and thunderstorm struck at approximately 5AM. Mother Nature spread into 4 large working brush and forest fires in the Lake Chelan area. These fires were named appropriately: The Chelan Butte Fire (AKA Reach One Fire) morphed into the Chelan Complex Fire; Deer Mountain and Antoine Creek Fire were included in this renaming.

Numerous people, homes, structures and community infrastructures were in harm's way.

FIRE STORM

Lightning bolts
    flashing down
        fires starting
            all around

Flames looming
    planes zooming
        tankers filling
            retardant spilling

Choppers flying
    people crying
        water falling
            loudspeakers calling

Evacuate
    get out, don't wait
        people fleeing
            fire sweeping

Power dead
    buildings red
        there is no light
            no help in sight

Phone not ringing
    birds not singing
        ash is choking
            trees are smoking

Nerves rattled
    Firemen battled
        tremendous heat
            dangerous feat

Embers rained
        uncontained
                as people cried
                        and three men died

Chelan Fires, August 14-28, 2015
By Maureen Taylor White

FIRE PERSONNEL

Chelan Fire and Rescue
Chelan, Douglas, Okanogan and Grant County Fire Departments
US Forest Service
Dept. of Natural Resources
Bureau of Land Management

Initial Attack (IA) operations took place from Aug-14, through August 15, 2015

Man hours: 2352

Extended operations: August 15 through August 28, 2015 and beyond; Man hours 1800

Fire mop up and recovery continued into late September, 2015

THUNDERSTRUCK

For as the lightning that comes from the east and is visible in the west, so will be the coming of the Son of Man; Matthew 24

Thunder and lightning! Abruptly awakened by a deafening jolt, my immediate thought was, *Jesus is that you?*

We lay motionless in the pre-dawn hours, listening to rolling thunder, accompanied by flashes of lightning pounding and pummeling the dry and thirsty Chelan Hills. Unaware of the forthcoming destructive event, I fell asleep once more and dreamed that I could hear the welcomed rains; the rain was only a dream. Friday; the morning of August 14th appeared uneventful when I drove into Chelan to do some grocery shopping and sundry errands. Arriving home that very hot afternoon, it was obvious that my flowers were languishing from thirst. Filling my watering can, I walked onto the front porch and noticed an ominous plume of smoke rising from the hills on the South shore directly across the lake from our Manson property. I called Denny to come for a look-see.

Finding our cameras, we began to snap a few pictures of the mounting plume. It was soon five o'clock, time to watch the news—oh, no television reception. With the power out, thought I'd rustle up some supper. Diving into a darkened refrigerator, not to let the cold out or the warm in, I quickly began to pull out cheese, salami and condiments for a sandwich to go with yesterday's leek and potato soup. Vichyssoise can be served cold!
As darkness fell we came to the awful realization that this power outage may take a while to repair. We've seen how fires have licked up electrical poles. This fire was probably caused by lightning strikes from the early morning "dry storm" which would be adding more stress to the overly burdened fire fighters and needed resources to combat many sinister fires growing in this area.

We are so addicted to being plugged in. One cannot really plan for a complete disconnect; can't wash clothes, can't run the dishwasher, and can't watch the news. But to top this, we had no phone service (land line or cell), and no computer. Forget enjoying a long hot shower.

Since we had front porch seating to view, what was called the Little Creek fire, we spent the evening watching our spectacularly devastating, seriously real, fireworks show, while the first pre-season Seahawk game became an insignificant distraction playing on our battery radio.

My husband can survive on a breakfast of *All-Bran* and *Trix* in a bowl of warm milk, but I don't do sawdust for breakfast. I needed protein. By now our refrigerator was at room temperature. "Let's do the ham, eggs and hash browns, before we have to throw them out," was my cheerful suggestion, even though I was well aware we didn't have natural gas or a charcoal barbeque grill or a camp stove. But we could build a fire in our *Jotul* wood burning stove that cozies our living room in the dead of winter.

"Build a fire in our stove?" With some consternation, Denny reminded me that this was August, and the outdoor temperatures, though thankfully somewhat cooler today, had been pushing into three digits much of this summer, and our central air needed electricity for cooling, and did I really want to heat up the house just to have a Watkins Cottage special?

"A hot cup of coffee could really minimize this dismal atmosphere," I whined. I reminded him of the propane burner, complete with caldron, stored in our garage; we've repurposed it for canning peaches. It had been used only once for our Thanksgiving turkey which was boiled in oil.

"Get the stuff together, I'll take the black cast iron skillet to the garage and torch the burner," he said somewhat reluctantly.

Breakfast served from our garage added a pinch of funny to this camping experience, yet the reality was that while sipping our hot cup of yesterday's coffee we watched the DC 10's make their retardant drops. I wondered about the unintentional fish fry as helicopters scooped up tons of water out of Lake Chelan to quell persistent flames.

Without the internet, television or telephone, or my husband's favorite pastime, the HAM amateur radio, which is supposed to keep us in communication with current and local disasters, except when the local relay tower is in flames—this was my chance, a game of Scrabble! I love playing Scrabble but had only out of town visitors to recruit. To commemorate this rare occasion, I took a picture of my husband playing Scrabble by candlelight—he's a good player!

The constant drone of planes and helicopters, heroically navigating in milky skies with severe wind gusts, brought a sense of security for us who lived across the lake from the inferno. I spent much of the day hoping and praying that homes of our friends and many evacuees on the South shore would be kept safe from the roiling smoke, which when darkness fell, revealed exploding flames that zigzagged down and across the hills keeping us mesmerized far past my bedtime.

The light in the hall woke me. The light in the hall—*thank you Lord.* It was Sunday, shortly after midnight.

One tends to think that being plugged in again would restore normalcy, but the fires continue to march across gulches and over ridges. Until I see my little Grands build a snowman in our yard, and until all peoples are safely tucked into their own beds again, can normalcy return?

Written by Grace Watkins

Five lightning strikes on the north face of Chelan Butte were accessible only by brush trucks. The winds headed west, then changed driving the wind to the east where it jumped the Chelan Gorge (Reach 1 Trail) heading to Chelan Falls (Reach 2-4) while moving north toward SR97A.

After jumping the Columbia River, it raced through the Douglas County side, specifically McNeil Canyon.

Once over the Reach 1 Trail ravine, the rest of the fire burned west toward the Lake Chelan Hospital, Deer Mountain and Union Valley (coming together with Antoine Creek Fire and Black Canyon Fires located behind the Chelan Airport).

Most of the homes, commercial and outbuildings were lost on this side of the ravine.

Chelan Complex Fires burned 88,985 acres, burning into Douglas and Okanogan County.

DUH
DON'T UNDERESTIMATE HYSTERIA

My neighborhood turned shockingly white around 5:15AM. Two blocks from my humble abode, lightning struck the arid hillside. The electrical charge immediately, and easily, consumed sage and bitterbrush. Orange flames charged west. Nervously, I gathered Jag and Saturian, assuring my cats the smoke was temporary. Overhead airplanes and helicopters repeatedly flew low, circling to drop water on the rapidly spreading fire. The ominous smoke and noise further unnerved the three of us.

Working from home, my heart rate settled into Level 2 Evacuation status, and my mind divided. Preoccupied, I continued to work greeting Realtors, providing technical support and answering common complaints. Tension mounted and my professional attitude wavered. Splitting my attention, I struggled with my own questions: Would my plan work? Would the pets wriggle into their carriers easily? Did I have everything needed in case the evacuation escalated? Intermittently, I gathered important articles from the house, placing them near the entrance to the garage. In preparation for the electricity to terminate, and to save time, I parked the car outside, nose positioned outward. The local radio station kept me informed and suggested items to pack; with each mention, I scurried to place them atop my outgoing pile.

Friday work schedule allowed an hour for lunch. I dined with a good friend who was also on Level 2. Full of Mexican food and hypothetical scenarios, I returned home satisfied. Twenty-three minutes later, a white car using a PA system announced, "Level 3 Evacuation Order in effect...Level 3 evacuation...leave your home now...do not wait for door-to-door notification. Evacuate immediately." The winds had changed, blowing east, directly toward my house.

My heart rate soared. Shaking, I sprang into action. Gathering the pile of belongings, I haphazardly tossed them into the back of my SUV, leaving the hatch open. The cat carrier door was open. With legs sprawled and head rigid, Saturian fought as I stuffed him inside. The cat carrier swayed as I raced around with it securing the house. Suddenly, the carrier's bottom detached, and my grey

9

guy went flying. We mirrored a look of shock though his face also confirmed mistrust—not what I needed at this time. I rushed to a blanket and tried to wrap him in it thinking, *he will fry, bad idea.* Immediately, I carried him to the car and tossed him in. Before I could close the hatch, he jumped out and ran under the deck—not what I needed at this time. Luckily, he ran to the other side of the deck, I grabbed him and placed him in the car's front seat and quickly closed the door behind him. Next, it was Jag's turn. Now, Jag is not my cat. He frequently attacks me. He was also suffering from an ear infection and not feeling well, but I couldn't bear to leave him. When I approached him, the look in his eyes reflected worry and hope. In one motion, I grabbed him by his hackles and scooped his weighty black body into my arms. Willingly or not, into the SUV's front seat he went. This was what I needed—a full car and cooperation.

Blocking their exit, I entered the car and drove off. It appeared that I was the only one evacuating; a police car had stopped a lengthy line of incoming vehicles. Once I was safely away from the subdivision, I drove to the ballpark and watched the flames stretch to reach my home. Aircraft sprayed the neighborhood with retardant. Embers and pink chemicals drifted over to the ballpark. Nervously, witnessing the protection of my residence, I strained to regroup my thoughts and tried to focus on a plan of action.

While the motor idled and the air conditioning blew, I watched my fuel levels drop. The cats whined in the background as my shaky hands made a few phone calls: Supervisor, Dad, both Nancy's and Al. Incoming calls: Katherine evacuated from Wal-Mart. Winds of 30mph caused the fire to rage down the Reach 1 Trail then leapt over the narrow river and swept up and over the ravine. Highway 150 was in its path as was Sandy's house. Immediately, I called her at work. She casually stated that she and her parents were just sitting around thinking about going home to check on things. I screamed, "Get home now! The fire's on its way!" Frightened, she agreed. Incoming calls: My supervisor, Dad, Al, Nancy and 2 co-workers. My phone's battery was depleting fast, showing a 35% charge.

Meanwhile, the fire consumed Reach 2 and 3, while winds carried flames toward Reach 4 and downward to Chelan Falls. More sirens blared as the fire jumped the mighty Columbia River—McNeil

Canyon blazed.

Catherine arrived at the ballpark. Fearing that the cats would bolt and through heavy smoke, we spoke between semi-lowered windows. Her Manson home was behind the fire to the north. She hoped her son, Corey, would make it home, as he worked in Entiat off Highway 97A. After reassuring her granddaughter that I was fine, they departed for their Manson house. I continued to watch the fire reach for fuel as cars came and went from the parking lot. I was pleased to see Corey's work truck pull in. I messaged Catherine that her son was on his way home; phone battery now 27%.

City power was down which meant no gas, no cash withdrawals and food soon would rot. I headed north to Purtteman Gulch. Nancy and Roger had fuel for me. When I arrived, the smoke was barreling down on their valley from the northeast. After parking near their newly purchased RV, I stepped out of my rig and I realized that I had no shoes on. I hugged Roger. That's when he told me their power was down. That meant: no fuel, no radio, no safe place. Nancy readied the RV. Roger loaded their five dogs into his vehicle. Nancy and I took off, driving toward her former brother-in-law's house located on the eastside of the ravine. Surely we could safely park the RV there. I rolled into his cul-de-sac. Flames reached over the ravine and black smoke filled the street. I yelled to Nancy, "It's too dangerous to park here, the fire's 20-feet away." She stammered something inaudible. That's when I panicked. My fuel was near empty. I roared over the neighbors and high winds, "I'm going to the City Marina—there's tarmac, water and green grass." Eventually, Nancy turned her RV around and followed me west.

With a watchful eye, sprinklers on and flashlight in hand, Roger had stayed home on Level 2 alert while Nancy and I spent the first night in the City Marina parking lot. Winds clocked at 45mph shook my car and the RV. Headlights shined through the windows all during the night, as onlookers parked to watch the fire heading west toward the Paradise View Condos. The First Creek fire raged northwest, glowing red-orange with flames reaching above Wapato Point Resort's peninsula. Only a few slept that night—pets included.

Twenty-four hours from the lightning's strike, Nancy and I headed up north to check on Roger where their Level 2 had escalated into Level 3. After a short visit, we waved him goodbye as he stayed to protect their property. We drove back to the RV.

Later that Saturday morning, I returned home—all was safe and standing though there was no power, food or gas. Nancy and Roger's Level 3 stirred ever-changing strategies and listening to the constant news reports added more tension. Catherine remained on Level 2. Sandy was not so fortunate. She watched as her home burned to the ground with just enough time to save her dog.

DUH

- Level 2; place your belongings IN the car!
- The above allows for calmly getting the pets into the car.
- Cat litter...hello!
- Cat food and water dishes, DUH!
- Don't put food down the kitchen drain...two days later you'll be asking, "who died?"
- Purchase a camp stove if you enjoy eating warm food.
- A crank radio with solar options, as information is a *must.*
- Headlamp for reading and searching for your flashlight...got batteries???
- Solar shower optional; after 3 days...what's that smell? Yikes!
- Put your toothbrush and paste IN your purse! Floss too.
- Pack credit cards, checks, insurance info and current outgoing bills.
- Pack Passport and Social Security card.
- Keep your cash close, what will you purchase when credit card system, fuel pumps and banks aren't available?
- Car phone charger...who ya gonna call with a dead battery?
- Fuel...your great escape, foiled again. Fire *will* win.
- Stay informed and be prepared.

Don't underestimate hysteria!

C. Marchi 8/2015

DEER MOUNTAIN FIRE

This fire became part of the Chelan Complex Fire in the Union Valley area which started from lightning strikes not accessible by road. The fire burned west to Union Valley Road coming together with the Antoine Creek Fire and burned west to the Black Canyon Fire. Three structures were lost in this area.

WATSON'S RESORT

Hello. I heard you [C. Marchi] on KOZI Radio and thought I might send you my notes on the First Creek Fire of Aug. 14th. While I am sure there are many wonderful and thankful stories you have received and heard about, our story is not quick like that, though we are thankful for many things. First and foremost is that we did not lose our business and family legacy here on the South Shore.

Also, I am sending this in its complete form. You may choose to remove some of the names involved in which I was not very happy with (if you choose to use this). As stated, these are my notes unedited.

If you have any questions, please let me know.

Robert Watson Jr.

Please know that I have the utmost respect for those men and women who are firefighters. This is not intended to degrade them in any way. What we have going on is a policy problem—problem at the top. So, here are my notes from the August 14th fire.

Part I

FIRST CREEK FIRE
AUG. 14TH, 2015

I think we all knew that the summer of 2015 was going to be a long, hot and dangerous fire season. We saw the signs early: low snow pack in the high mountains, no snow pack down low, and a spring that arrived early. About three or four weeks early around the North Central Washington area and this trend continued into summer. We saw 90 degree temps early in May, which was also much earlier than normal. We knew. And then, the rains stopped.

Knowing that things would be bad concerning wild fires and after seeing what happen in the Carlton Complex Fire last summer, here at Watson's Resort we prepared early for a bad year. We hoped it would not arrive but planning in the event that it did. We cleared old roads on the hill and even made new roadways as fire breaks. We got our water system going early and activated permanent water lines and sprinklers. Big Gun sprinklers were running high up on the hill. We mowed brush and grass. Throughout the summer, we continued to prepare. Mowing sections of the old orchard land as firebreaks. And then, it happened.

August 14th, 2015.

Note - Times are all approximate times.

5:30AM - I had just stepped out the door of our house and was going to head up on the hill to do some more mowing. Thunder could be heard in the distance. I was walking toward my truck when a large bolt of lightning lit up the Western skies. It was bold. It was blinding bright, and it was immediately followed by a crack and boom of thunder. It was close. Right over the top, of what we call *Prospect Mountain*—the mountain just above our old orchard. It was big and it hit close and I knew it was a strike.

5:35AM - Rather than heading to the orchard to mow, I drove up to the hair pin corner by McCulley's and noticed smoke on the hill just above Don Castles place—about two thirds of the way up the mountain. I immediately called in the fire and was told that it had already been reported though the radio announced later that it was not reported until after 6am. We had us a fire in our back yard. Perhaps our fears for months were coming true.

I sat and watched for a while. While watching, I saw another strike behind Manson and then one that appeared to be up lake around Slide Ridge or Fields Point or at least in that direction. And there seemed to be a lot of activity in the Chelan area. I drove down to the resort and checked the Doppler Radar. A large cell was over the top of the lower Chelan Valley heading North by Northeast toward the Pateros/Brewster area.

6:45AM - Adam and Steve (two of our employees) arrive to work and we went over our game plan for the day. I told them that we would rotate sprinklers on the hill about every two hours. We wanted to get as much wet as we could, since Red Flag wind warnings were in the forecast for the afternoon.

8:00AM - I headed up to the old orchard and proceeded to mow in what used to be called the 1st planting of the orchard. We mowed around the Big Gun settings on top. Adam and Steve continued to change the water settings throughout the morning.

Throughout the morning, I continued to monitor fires around the Chelan Valley. My oldest son Bo said that there was a fire just behind his house on the Butte but he was working in Wenatchee at the time. They live in South Chelan just below the water tower. I continued to drive around watching the First Creek Fire and noticed that there wasn't one but two fires burning on the mountain above the orchard. The one I saw at 5:35am and one on the very top of Prospect Mountain. And winds were forecasted to pick up in the afternoon.

Around 11:30AM - Figured it could be a long night so I took a half hour nap—little did I know.

2:00PM - On the hill with Big Gun lines and mowing.

3:30PM - I called Adam and Steve to come back out to help; they had gone home for the day. I told Steve to key on the resort and Adam on the hill. Steve got sprinklers going on my parent's house and at the barn. My youngest son, Donny, crawled up on the Lodge roof and began hand watering down the roof.

I also went to the Alpenhorn and told the kids working there to put away the new stock that Sysco had just delivered, do a quick clean up and close down and leave.

Lost power at resort about this time but did not know it as I was up on the hill.

4:00PM - Went to orchard to fight fire up there.

4:30PM - Called and spoke with Donny. He was sitting on the top of the Lodge roof and did not know how to get down. When he went up the shingles were dry. After hosing down the roof, the shingles were wet and slick. I called Steve to get Donny a ladder so he could get down off the roof.

Fire was now to the outside of the fence so I headed up with the John Deere tractor to make fire line on the old road on the outside of the fence. Things were looking good except for one small area where it had gotten below the old road. The ground was bone dry so I could not get off the old road in fear of burying the tractor in the powder dry dirt. I continued to clear the old road until oldest son, Bo, came up and told me that I needed to head down. He said that there were some fire fighters at the mill site and they said that they were going to start a back burn. I hated to leave as I was making good work with the tractor but I headed down to see what was going on.

There did not seem to be any interest from the crew of about eight or ten to go out and try to stop the fire—even the section I was working in. I explained to them that I had cut a pretty good line on the old road and it seemed to be holding, that if a couple of them could cut a line on the upper and lower sides by hand, this fire would be looking pretty good. I asked the guy in charge if they were going to go up and look at it and he said that they were not. I told him that the roadway was safe as we had watered everything and that he could drive up there. He said that he had driven to the corner (about halfway up) and that was far enough for him. Nothing was done.

I ask the guy in charge if they were going to back burn the hill and he said that they were not going to do it right away. So I said, "So, I am safe to head back up there?" and he said that I was fine for the time being. So, I told him, "Me and my Deere (John Deere Tractor) are going to go fight some fire. I headed back up the hill.

Later, I was told that three of the forest service persons were walking up the hill after I left, carrying canisters to do the back burn. I am not sure where they went. I never saw them.

Prior to going back up with the tractor, I sent Zaron (a friend) and Adam down to go start getting ready to move the horses out. We hooked up the trailer, and got the horses out. Zaron said that we could move them to his family's place over at Manson, which we really appreciated.

I checked the firebreak I had made and it was looking pretty good, except where it had crossed the road. I looked up on the hill and noticed a fire going and a tree crowning at the very top of what used to be the Gala planting. This is the hill between us and First Creek. I quickly drove the tractor to the top to see what the fire was doing. Not as bad as it looked from down below but not good either and there was really not much I could do up there. I came back down the hill. I was amazed that there was fire up there as there was not fire near that area a few minutes earlier. When I came back down I noticed smoke over by our neighbors to the East, the Powers residence. Here again, I was amazed that fire was over there. I took the tractor over there and proceeded to try and cut a line there. Then I noticed smoke from below Powers house. This was between Powers house and Shadow Bay Belgians. It was time to head toward the resort and barn. I parked the tractor at the mill and headed down. It was time to make sure the horses were moved out and key on the barn and resort.

Leaving the mill area was not a huge concern for there was a fire crew there. I think we all thought the mill would be Ok.

It was about this time that a Forest Service person met with my wife, Socco. He had a map and indicated to her that all the cabins up lake from Watson's and Watson's Resort itself would burn and that she needed to leave NOW. Socco, with the help of friend Jody and Tenant Mr. Zenk, loaded things into the car and went to the Alpenhorn to wait there.

6:00PM - Pulled out of orchard and headed down to the barn.

6:15PM- Loaded horses. Zaron and Adam took horses to Sandem's place. Fire crossed the highway above Cabins #1, 2, 3 and 4. Socco and kids headed to town and said they would be at Harrisons'.

6:30PM - I was speaking with a Forest Service person on the highway. Nothing was being done by those up on the road. Lots of watching and picture taking by fire personnel. I explained that the fire had jumped the road and was above some of our cabins. In the middle of the conversation, the guy I was talking to got all excited and took off running in an up lake direction. I was wondering what had happened. This guy proceeded to run about 15 or so feet and started taking pictures of trees that were burning and crowning up lake from the intersection and above the highway. He was taking pictures with his cell phone. I thought, *"What the heck is going on here?*" He seemed more concerned about getting a good photo than dealing with what I had to say or dealing with the fire.

It was later that we found out that some other firefighters had been taking Facebook Selfie shots. Big fire in the background and them with smiling faces. Clean as a whistle. All this happened while the fire was burning behind our cabins.

About this time, Bo (my oldest son) and I got a couple shovels and headed down to the resort. We rounded the corner and saw fire directly behind Cabin #3, which is Betty Mickey's cabin. I remember telling Bo that I did not think we would be able to stop this fire. That we were going to lose those cabins. I kept thinking about Mrs. Mickey and how happy she was with the newly remodeled cabin. I would hate to have to tell her that her cabin burned down.

Bo and I proceeded to the back of Cabin #3. Power was out, and our water system at the resort was drained. No water. All we had was shovels and dirt so we proceeded to shovel dirt onto the fire, which was on the bank three feet from the cabin. Shoveling dirt into brush just does not work very well and I really did not think we had much of a chance but after a while, it seemed to be working. We were gaining on it. The hot spots and flames were getting a little smaller. Within a half hour or so, Cabin #3 was looking pretty good as was Cabin #4.

7:15PM - I drove back up to the intersection and smoke with a Forest Service person. I pleaded with him to get us some help. I told him if he could just give us two guys with shovels, I thought we could save these cabins. He told me that he would see what he could do. I went back down to help Bo. Things looked good behind Cabins #3 and #4. I moved them to the back of Cabin #2 where it was kind of flaring up. We could hear voices on the highway above us. Bo and I kept yelling out for help to send down some help. Nobody came.

It was shortly after this that two Sheriff's came down to the resort. One of them yelled out "Are you guys Ok?" I told them that we were OK but that we need some help with the fire. One of the Sheriffs walked to where he could see me and told me that I did not look very good and that I needed to get some water. So Bo and I went down to the lake. We rinsed off our faces. Took a few drinks of lake water then walked back to the back side of the cabins. On the way back one of the Sheriffs said to me, "Do you know that you are not going to put out that fire with a shovel and a little bit of dirt?" This comment really upset me and I turned to the Sheriff and said something like, "Look Buddy. We just saved two cabins with "A Little Bit of Dirt" and if you would get us some help down here we could save these cabins and the resort." Bo and I returned to working on the fire while the two Sheriffs stood in the lawn area for 30 minutes or so watching us. No help. Not getting us help—just watching with their arms crossed.

7:45PM - A truck with a pump and hose finally arrived. Bo and I were thrilled to see this. We helped them get the hose out and they started spraying water. Not really where it was needed but water nevertheless. After maybe two minutes or so, the guys walked back to the truck and said that they had to leave. I asked them why and they said that they were to pull out. I asked them why again and they said that they were ordered to pull out and that something was heading our way. He said that there was going to be a wall of fire coming down on us. He said that we could expect to see lots of fire and embers in the air and coming down on us. They packed up and left. It was such a great feeling when they arrived but so very disappointing to see them leaving so quickly.

8:00PM - Donny (my youngest son) and Caleb (a high school employee of ours) showed up. Here again it was such a great feeling to have some additional help. Caleb worked the high side of Cabin #4. I put Donny on the up lake side of Cabin #1. I showed Donny how to cut a line while using the dirt to try and put out the fire above him. Things were looking better but I had a concern with Cabin #1. Fire was approaching from the up lake side and there was a lot of brush between the fire and the cabin. I went to get the chainsaw and loppers, and also, drove back up on the road. I told a guy up there again that we needed help. That guy directed me to a fellow in charge.

I ask the person in charge why he pulled the pump truck out from the resort. He told me that he was not going to put the lives of his men in danger. That he was not going to risk their lives. I explained to him that things were safe down at the resort. That his men would not die. I told him that I had my two sons and a high school employee down there and that I would never place their lives in danger.

The fellow in charge just looked at me and said, "I am not going to do it."

So I asked him if he had even been down to the resort? He said that he had not. I told him to drive down and at least look at the place and that he would see that it was safe. I told him that there was a large grass area and lots of lake. I told him his men would not die or get hurt.

He said, "I am sorry but I am not sending anyone down there."

I was now very upset so I asked him his name.

He replied by saying, "What is your name?" kind of in a smart ass way.

I gave him my name and asked his name again. He gave me his name. So I said to him, "If you are not going to use your shovels, could we borrow two??

He said, "No."

I looked at him and said, "Thank God our military does not fight wars the way you fight fires." This really upset him, but at that point, I really did not care. I could tell that we were not going to get any help and that we were on our own. We were not getting help from anyone. I had not seen a sign of anyone from District #7 Chelan or South Shore. If the resort was going to be saved, it would have to be saved by us. I left to go help Bo, Donny and Caleb.

8:00PM or 8:30PM - It was dusk but hard to tell the exact time. A family in a boat had been watching the fire from the lake. They yelled in to us and asked if we needed any help. Bo replied that we did so the family brought their boat into the dock and tied up. I think the Mother stayed on the boat while the Father and two or three kids helped with a bucket brigade of water. Dan and Daniel Goodfellow, neighbors to the east, also showed up and helped out. I thought to myself - We have tourists from Wapato Point helping us and neighbors helping us but we have a bunch of paid employees on the road that will not even set foot into the resort. This was actually very touching to me. The tourists that is, not the guys on the road.

Judging from photos I have seen, it may have been about this time that our orchard shed burned down as well as our up lake neighbors (Senator Parlette).

8:30PM - Finally for the first time I saw a Fire Personnel in a pickup drive down into the resort and make a loop around the cabins. Perhaps, it was the fellow in charge whom I upset. He drove in and around and left without stopping but at least we saw something.

9:00PM or 9:30PM - A one-ton rig arrived with pumps and hose and proceeded to get set up with a floating pump. It had been about three or four hours since the fire had jumped the road above the cabins before we got any help. The fire behind the cabins was in pretty good shape—under somewhat control. My concern was still the up lake side of Cabin #1 and the bank heading up toward the barn but with this crew here, we were able to kind of relax.

We continued checking things up on the road and watching for new starts. Throughout that night and clear into the dawn of morning, we kept seeing the homes up lake burn. Now many think that the fire swooped down on those homes and they burned all at once. That was not the case. A different home went up in flame about every hour or so. We could easily see the glow and black smoke from the resort when another summer home caught fire. I really do not know if much was being done to keep them from burning.

The crew that showed up to help us about 9:30pm or so did great work. They worked hard all night long. Cut brush. Dug a line. Watered things down. They worked all night long, took a quick nap then headed out to another place. These are the guys and gals we say thank you to. As for the fellow in charge and the bunch on the highway, I was very disappointed in them that first night.

I realize that this was one hell of a hell storm. Things happen so fast and resources were spread thin. I realize this. But there were people around. They were on the road at the entrance to our resort. They just would not do anything.

I will continue my notes another day but this is the jist of what happen on Aug. 14th.

We do thank all those brave men and women out there who work so hard fighting fires. We saw some of them at work that night and you should all be proud of the outstanding work you do. Thank you all very much, but policy needs to change. The policy we have now is not working. We need to bring back some logging and grazing in our forests. Open up roadways for dealing with fires. This helps our forests a bit. Not that we will not have forest fires. We will always have forest fires, but something needs to change.

Part II

Good Morning. It's time for part two, where I will take off from where I left off last night. Yesterday's notes covered the first day of the fire on August 14th. This section will cover Aug. 15th and on. So if you did not read the first day notes, now is a good time to do that.

Throughout the night, we would drive up to the intersection. Fire was around our resort water reservoir and we watched that from time to time hoping it would not get hot enough to damage the bladder inside the tank. At this time, the fire was pretty much down to the highway from First Creek all the way up lake. I saw a lot of men and lots of standing but really nothing being done. At one point, I heard a pump fire up and a truck proceeded to drive up the road and water down the ditch. I thought, *what the heck.* The fire had burned all the way down to the ditch and road and they were going to put out the fire in the ditch but did not come down to help us? Just did not make sense to me.

August 15th

1:30AM – Noticed a hot fire up by Doug's Mill. This is the mill that was on the property on the hill in our old orchard. It was hot, large flames, but no black smoke. As near as I could tell, it was the big log

24

pile on the Chelan side of the mill.

2:00AM - Noticed a lot of black smoke coming from the mill pile. I figured Doug's camper and the mill building was going up (or both). We also heard two explosions. One was most likely a propane tank in Doug's camper. Not sure what the other explosion was. And I was sure that we had lost both tractors and Doug's boom—very sad.

Drove up to the highway and noticed someone finally went up to check on our neighbors, the Powers house. Was not sure how it had fared the night.

2:30 to 4:00AM - I slept in my Dad's truck down by the pool with Donny and Bo. Bo slept a bit longer than I did and Donny longer than Bo. It was after I woke up at 4:00am that I could still see a cabin catching fire up lake. This continued into the twilight hours of morning. It was so sad as it seemed a house burned up every hour or so and it seemed that there was nothing being done to stop them.

When it was light enough to see, I walked out on our dock and was thrilled to see that the Powers house was still there. It was early but I had to call and tell them for I knew that they would be worried all night long.

Sometime during the morning, I drove up to the intersection and spoke with the Sheriff. I explained to him that we had a large gravity flow water line that came from First Creek and expressed my concern with it having a break and leaking water. I told him it could be a real mess if it was leaking water. I asked him if I could go to the orchard on the hill about ¼ mile up lake and check on it. He said no. He said that I could not go beyond the barricade. I explained the seriousness of this but he would not budge. I then looked at him and told him I was not sure whom the liability would fall on but in my opinion, if something happen, he would be liable and responsible. Not me. I told him that I was just trying to help prevent a further problem. He said something to the affect "so be it."

The pump rig pulled out of the resort around 10am or so. Those guys and gals did a great job that night. Watered things down and cut lines. Moved things, cut brush, etc.. Hats off to them, but unfortunately, they were called elsewhere and, once again, we were on our own. There was still smoke and fire below the road but at least it has a good line around it.

Doug, Bo and Zaren all walked to the mill site. About a half hour later I hear something on the highway. It was Doug's boom rig. It survived the fire. I then heard a tractor. It was the John Deere. IT survived. Then I heard a third. The Ford tractor made it. That was a great sound to hear all three of those rigs heading down the highway.

I tried again later in the day with another Sheriff to go check the water line on the hill. I was very concerned about having a major wash out up on the hill and having a wall of water and mud coming down the hill and blocking the highway. Unfortunately, I was told the same thing by that Sheriff that was on duty that evening. I could not go check. They never offered to make a call or to send someone up with me to check things out. My concern was a washout that could close the South Shore Road, but their only concern was not letting anyone cross the road block.

August 16th

6:00AM - I drove the John Deere up the back road of the resort to check the water line. I tried to do it the right way by asking at the road block, which did not work, so I did it my way. I drove clear to the top and noticed two areas just above the 1st planting that had pipeline failures and were putting out a large amount of water. I drove below the leaks and while attempting to cross where the water was running, buried the tractor in mud clear up over the front tires and halfway up the back tires. I had to walk down off the hill to the resort. That soil was building up with water and it was only a matter of time before it cut loose, and now it had a tractor in it too.

I then drove up to the intersection. The Sheriff was on the road and I spoke with him about the broken water line. I told him my concern with the orchard soil giving out, sliding down and blocking the entire county road. He made a phone call and received permission for us to go up First Creek and pull the pipe and then go up on the hill and retrieve the tractor, which we did. Hats off to that Sheriff. He did the right thing. Made a call and got permission. Another Sheriff and the other staff would not do anything—just saying, " NO." Very disappointed in them.

Since the pump truck had left on the morning of the 15th, we had to haul buckets of water up the hill to keep the fire in check that was burning below the highway. This was above Cabin #4 and #5 and below the Barn Condo.

August 17th

2:00AM – After more than 50 hours without ever seeing anyone drive into the resort to help or check on things, we finally saw a fire crew stop on the County road above the resort and worked on the fire that was burning between the cabins and the Barn Yard Condo (Barn Trailer). Prior to this (Saturday, Sunday and Monday) we had been carrying buckets of water from the lake up the hill to keep the fire from flaring up. This was a DNR crew and they were great; hats off to these fire fighters.

Power was restored this evening. So now we had our water back and the system was OK. I was concerned about the bladder in the tank.

August 18th

1:00AM – Got about three hours sleep and woke up at 1:00AM. At 2:00am I was out checking our water system and wanted to release air out of facets at the barn and check the reservoir for leaks.

There was a State Trooper and a Sheriff at the intersection. I approached them in my truck at 2:00am and the Trooper walked up to me. I explained to him that we had just gotten power and I was checking our water system and asked if I could drive past the barrier about 50-feet to our barn entrance to check water. He said that I could not travel beyond the barrier. I again explained that I was only asking to go 50-feet and I told him "right at the sign" (pointing to the sign fifty feet up the road).

He again said no.

I said, "Well fine, I will just go through this gate" (pointing to the gate by the resort sign but down lake from the barricade).

He said, "No you will not."

Which I replied, "Like hell I won't." I told him that his barricade was there (pointed to barricade) and the gate was here (pointing to the gate which was not past the barrier). I told him I was not breaking his barricade and that he could not keep me out. He asked who I was and told him. I asked if he wanted to see ID and he said that he did. I showed it to him. I then said, "This is bullshit."

The Sheriff then said, (referring to me), "You are right. This is bullshit."

Throughout the morning, I proceeded to go in and out of the gate checking things as well as checking the reservoir on the hill until Steve and Adam showed up, then they took over.

Midday – Finally saw a pickup drive in the resort and make a round. Today we worked on watering the banks above the cabins and below the barn.

August 19th

9:00AM – The DNR guys that helped put out the fire below the Barn Condo drove down into the resort. Steve talked to them and then I did. They asked if I remembered them and I said they did. We chatted for a spell and one of them said, "We are so sorry. We had no idea all this was down here." He then gave me a telephone number and said if we had any type of problem what so ever, to call that number. They were very nice and helpful young men. They seemed to truly care and feel bad unlike most others we had to deal with.

A day or two later, Socco, Mandy and Hayley went for a walk up to the orchard and this same DNR crew was up there putting out hot spots. Socco and Mandy told me how nice they were and how bad they felt about all our problems and all the loss we had from the fire. They offered the gals water and were just very nice guys. THANK YOU FIRE FIGHTERS.

August 21st

Day 8 - All well. I have been allowed to drive 50-feet to the barn for watering and feeding the last two days. Yes, the horses returned home.

Cindy Goodfellow informed me tonight that there has been some looting going on.

Removed barriers on the road and set up blockage tonight and moved them to the Yacht Club.

These are my notes of what happen those first few days. Like so many others, I wish that I could have put up a sign that said, "Thank you Firefighters" but on Aug. 14th, when we needed help and there were guys around, we were left on our own. I am so thankful and proud to have had my two sons by my side that night as well as that outstanding young man Caleb.

As stated, there are outstanding men and women out there who do óutstanding work. We saw some of them later that night on Aug. 14th and several days later, but we also saw the other side which most may not hear about.

So that is kind of what happened to us out here at Watson's Resort during the fires. Some fire persons who would not do anything to help and some Law Enforcement people who had attitudes—very unfortunate. As for me, Ya, I know my fuse was short. But aren't they supposed to be the professionals?

29

Oh, and by the way, it has been about 6 weeks since that Aug. 14th fire night. I called and spoke with Fire District's Chief on Aug. 24th with some questions for him. He was to get back to me. I have not seen or heard from him in over a month. Have yet to see a District 7 or South Shore Fire rig in here at Watson's.

But here we are. We made it and have seen some better days since. Thank you to those DNR crews who were so very helpful and caring. Thank you to all our tenants and guests who have been so thankful. Thank you to our employees. Have I ever said what great employees we have? Thank you to so many friends who helped out. So very much to be thankful for.

Written by Robert Watson Jr.

ANTOINE CREEK FIRE

This fire became part of the Chelan Complex Fire and started north of Quiet Valley in Okanogan County from lightning strikes and was not accessible by road. The fire burned down into Antoine Creek destroying a number of homes/buildings before reaching Washington Creek and coming together with the Deer Mountain fire on the north side of Union Valley.

MAKE A DIFFERENCE DAY
By Mark Tesch

Red delicious apples, shiners picked from the trees
water-cored and sweet.
Golden delicious, baked on the fringes of the orchards,
left to hang.

Autumn painted leaves on trees which did not burn.
Charred black stumps of those that did.

Baseball teams and Rotarians,
Lutherans and the Lions' Club.
Chelan Valley Help and Habitat neighbors.
All step up.

Much was lost here,
More than pole barns and tractors.
More than homes and dreams.
More than...

But not all was lost.
NO! Not all was lost.
Grasses spring up through the charcoal tuffs of grass,
before the winter snows fall.
Trailer homes for the victims are winterized and made ready.
New fences are stretched across the orchard boundaries,
across the endless miles of nature, meeting mankind of its own
terms.

Much was lost here.
But rebuilding is restoring hope.
Sunny smiles on a grey day bring joy and consolation.
Volunteers made a difference.

But there is no illusion that all is well,
or back to normal.

Normal will be redefined.
We can only wait, with hope, for solidarity of Spirit.
There is no illusion that it will be easy.

FROM THE ASHES

Our cabins have survived more than one fire, and have had some mighty close calls. But, August 14th gave us the perfect storm; severe drought conditions, excessive temperatures, dry lightning and high winds. When nature screams this loud, all we mere mortals can do is get out of the way. It was another week before we were able to talk our way past the guard on South Shore Road so we could see what remained. He let us walk in since our place was less than a quarter mile away. What a surreal walk that was; open flames shooting through tree stumps and knotholes, charred wood, dead trees and smoke everywhere. All the way in I was hoping to see remains of something the flames may have missed, but as I looked out toward the lake from the hill where the cabins had been I saw there was nothing left but thick smoky ash and rubble. No color anywhere—just blacks and grays. The feeling was indescribable as we hugged each other and let the tears come.

There had been three cabins, a garage, carport and playhouse. As you began the climb down the trail to the lake, you would first see the two-car garage over a large workshop. Then walk down two switchbacks to another little cabin, one large room and a bathroom. A water tank situated behind it to ensure water could make it to the top of the hill. Then down two more switchbacks to our sleeping cabin, four bedrooms and a bathroom. And on down the final switchback to the main cabin which consisted of two more small bedrooms, a kitchen with grandma's old Monarch woodstove (I had my first cooking lessons there), dining area and living room, done up in knotty pine except the living room which had been added on some years later. An outdoor flight of stairs took us down to the patio and dock area by the lake. There were also two basements below the main cabin, one for the water heater, pump, tools, sink and makeshift shower, and one for storage.

All of these cabins were built over a period of nearly fifty years. Five generations now have considered it "home." In this age of mobility, where it is a rare occurrence to find a home that has housed several generations of the same family, the cabins have been our touchstone - the place we come to reflect and rejuvenate, to set aside petty squabbles and reset our life's priorities. It has been there for us through births and deaths, marriages and divorces, wartime and peacetime, and the good years and bad.

The memories that linger on this now barren property are powerful. Parents, grandparents and great grandparents' letters, pictures, handmade treasures, the dollhouse my grandfather made for me nearly seventy-years ago, grandma's quilts and crochets, great grandparents souvenirs, the World War I cavalry hat and spurs, the yoke that came with them from Holland in the 1800's, granddad's prize-winning deer head along with the bear, several antlers and the mountain goat. My grandfather, Tony, was the driving force behind the cabins. This was his legacy to the family, and he would have been heartbroken to have seen it completely destroyed. But the legacy he actually left was much more than the buildings or the beautiful property on the lake. All of our hearts have been touched by the work, the care and the love that was put into it by our grandparents and parents.

I have begun a list of the items we have been able to salvage from these four buildings and eighty-years of mementoes. So far, we have found a blackened plate, teapot, doorknob, three bent wheels from a toy wagon, tines from the rake, a nutcracker, and a charred piece of newspaper burned into the shape of a heart with the word *family* printed on it. We have no idea what to do with these things, but it is somehow comforting to have found them.

Miraculously under the ashes, the dock, patio and stone fireplace still stand, giving us a fitting place for a new start. This is where we spent our time - outdoors by the lake; diving off the dock, nights in front of the fireplace, midnight skinny dipping, s'mores, barbecues, the big dipper, contemplating the stars, marveling at the Milky Way, and tons of music and laughter. The cabins were for sleeping and shelter from bad weather, but our days and nights were spent outside on the dock or in front of the fireplace. So, we already have a place to begin. All we need now is time. Time to honor the memories of the past; we'll begin new ones. And to treasure that simple charred word *family* which somehow survived the intense heat and flames to remind us of what is truly important.

Written by Nancy Culp

Fire personnel busied themselves with multiple fire assessments,
equipment and resource management while saving structures and lives.
Included are condensed notes from their minute-by-minute reports.

06:36 *First Creek Fire reported*
06:52 *Slide Ridge Fire reported; 06:52 (Chelan Fire and Rescue B73 (4)*
head to Chelan Cellars
06:57 *Command 703 - they have eyes on the fire, not accessible by*
vehicle, they are waiting on the air tankers to arrive, probably a couple
of hours out. CC7 and CWICC are monitoring the fires until then
07:37 *Request Law Enforcement to Station 71, may have to start doing*
evacuations in the Hawks Meadow area.
07:40 *(DNR) placed an order through CWICC for a type 1 or type 2*
aircraft. I made numerous attempts ordering resources through
CWICC with the same response of "none available."
07:40 *Wolverine has a T1 and T3 available of IA, contact tanker base*
and they will work to get the folks in early.
07:58 *USFS and DNR at the First Creek Fire.*
Chelan Fire and Rescue then responded to the First Creek Fire which
was found to be burning at the top of one of the ridges and appeared
to be very small in size. Forest service units were in the area including
DNR. Those units said they would be taking that incident as it was
well outside of our protection district and not accessible by our crews.
07:58 *Chelan Fire and Rescue Command First Creek Fire, headed to*
Granite Falls to assess the fire.

JOAN LESTER'S STORY
September 11, 2015

Thoughts regarding the recent fires:

  I have lived in the Chelan valley for most of my life, so I always assumed I would be in no personal danger from forest or brush fires.

  I assumed we would be protected by the perimeter of irrigated orchards surrounding the communities of Chelan and Manson and by the lake itself.

  I assumed we could place a boat in the lake and escape the fires, or, if we had no boat, we could walk to the lake and wade in to the cold water.

  This year I learned the fire could be spread across the lake by intense wind, so the lake itself was no barrier. The irrigated land also could be crossed by embers carried by the wind.

  To use a boat, you must have a working boat, the ability to transport the boat to the water and the gas to move both the boat and the vehicle pulling the boat to the water.

  And then on a more personal level, I am no longer able to walk to the shore or maneuver while standing in the cold water.

  Manson, where I live, had no telephones because the poles had burned. There was no radio because the transmitters had been burned. There was no television because those transmitters had burned. There was very thick smoke so you could not see the hill on the other side of the lake and could not tell the fires' progress.

  Therefore, when we heard that the community had the highways to the north and the south closed by fire activity, I chose not to be trapped in Manson. On Friday evening, my son drove his family and myself through Chelan and to Wenatchee. Every motel in Wenatchee was full. Several gas stations were out of fuel.

We were lucky, we had relatives to stay with.

I guess you could say my husband's brother and his wife were lucky because they, too, had relatives in Wenatchee to take them in. But in their case, their home had been burned to the ground. They lived on Columbia View road in Chelan. The fire had to travel from the Butte on the south shore of Lake Chelan, across the Chelan River and across a highway to reach their home. But it did, and with such speed that they were able to escape with only their clothes, one dog and one cat. They had been providing housing for my grandson and his mother, so they, too, lost their belongings.

I spent three nights in Wenatchee because I was scared.

However, we should try to look for something good in everything. The good I have seen was in the response of the people here to help those hurt by the fires. I have two examples.

My husband and I took our 10-year-old grandson to the ice cream store at River Walk Park. We were talking to the girl dispensing ice cream about how Wyatt had lost all his toys to the fire. A little while later, she approached me and quietly offered me a carefully folded twenty-dollar bill with the whispered instructions to by Wyatt some toys. At first, I hesitated. But when she said, "Please, please." I realized this was important to her; she was expressing her sympathy.

The next day, my husband had occasion to be in the Art Gallery on Main Street. He wandered in to look at the painting and, finding some by a local artist Rod Weagant. He commented to the gallery operator that his brother had three Weagant paintings on his walls when his house burned. The young woman picked up a Weagant print and handed it to my husband with instruction to give it to his brother. The young woman was Mr. Weagant's daughter, and she too was expressing sympathy of their loss.

MY TRANSISTOR RADIO

The first patent of the transistor radio was filed in Canada by Austrian-Hungarian physicist Julius Edgar Lillenfeld on October 22, 1925.

My parents handed down this antique radio to me. Before the fires started, I had gone to Kelley's Hardware Store in Chelan to purchase new batteries for it. This turned out to be one of my best decisions.

Several days later, fires swept the Lake Chelan Valley. Being born and raised here I had never seen fires of this nature. Back in 1995, before I moved back to Manson and when my Mother was alive, there were severe fires that year. She said the smoke was so thick that she could not see across the lake. She did not have to evacuate. Bravely, she stayed home until the smoke cleared.

With the fire season of 2015, I was living in Manson and working in Chelan. That Friday afternoon while at work, we opened the back door to watch the airplanes spray flame retardant in the area of Chelan High School.

Then I went home and watched the fires continue to spread into the Chelan State Park area, Watson's Resort and up lake and higher into the mountains. I did not have to evacuate from my home.

I was lucky to have had my transistor radio with new batteries. KPQ radio station in Wenatchee provided excellent coverage of the fires as well as Public Radio. Kozi, our local radio station, did not have power for a time. I was told the PUD eventually brought them a power device so they could continue serving our area. I was without electricity for many hours. I was told others went to Wenatchee and stayed with friends and family or in hotels to escape the effects of these horrific fires.

I have some life-long friends whose homes burned in this fire. They have had to pick up the pieces and start over again.

Better times ahead for all Lake Chelan residents.

I am so thankful to have my transistor radio, which sits on my kitchen counter. Being informed helped to settle my nerves.

ADDITIONAL ASSISTANCE

08:19 Chelan County Sheriff's Officer Department of Emergency Management requested

08:30 Helicopter operations taking place on the Chelan Butte

08:51 Red Cross has been notified, they are working on shelters

THE GOOD SAMARITANS

Phone glued to my ear, I was supervising the unloading of 16 residents of our assisted living facility in Chelan into their evacuation center at the Red Lion Inn in Wenatchee and setting up transport of one resident whose care needs could not be met at the evacuation center and needed to be hospitalized. The air was smoky, residents were understandably disoriented as they disembarked the Link bus vans and lined up with their various mobility assistance devices and waited for our banquet room, our temporary home, to be made ready. A couple approached and asked to speak with me.

It had been another worldly-surreal-frightening and busy-with-no-sleep 36 hours since the lightning strikes on the Butte set off the chain of events that sent us to the Red Lion. In that other world, I had a warm secure bed and awoke next to my sweetheart to the sound of thunder at about 5AM the day before. It was the first day of the Lake Chelan Arts Festival. For the festival we create a children's area complete with a large cardboard castle to paint and play on and crowns to decorate and wear. This year was to be the debut of Spike, the Wolverine dragon, a large, mostly finished, papier mache 12- foot long dragon with 8 foot wingspan. We had supplies for children to help us apply the finishing touches to Spike throughout the 3-day weekend festival. We went down to Riverwalk Park as planned, setting up for opening at 9am, and always with an eye on the Butte. By midday, it was obvious that we were going to be needed at the assisted living facility, so we closed up our area, tethered Spike to the castle and headed up the hill to Heritage Heights where I am a nurse and my sweetheart handles maintenance. Evacuations for the affected areas of Chelan were well underway and staffing was in turmoil, so we pitched in as needed and just after supper the power went off.

Dark descended and the fire spots on the Butte looked like city lights. Our administrator brought her two parrots to work for their safety (her home was evacuated later that evening) and they quickly learned to mimic the sound of the alarm, telling us the power was out. Residents, accustomed to retiring to their rooms for TV, were a little lost. At one point, I found several residents in the fireplace room in the glow of flashlights circled up around the coffee table upon which sat the two parrots in their cages. Bedtime was earlier for most, care was challenging by the light of headlamps and by 9pm most all were bedded down in the eerie glow of the fires across the way. Several of us spent the night because with no power the fire alarm system and the nurse call system were not operational and minimum hourly checks were required. With dawn came uncertainty, do we stay or go? By midmorning, the decision was made to evacuate. Families were notified; those that were able, collected their loved ones and the rest were very thankful we could care for them at the shelter. Within an hour of the decision, families and EMT personnel arrived and the evacuation went very smoothly. Residents were loaded onto three Link vans. Food, medications, medical records and small bags of personal belongings for each resident were rapidly packed and loaded. Within an hour and a half of the decision, we pulled away bound for Wenatchee.

Returning to the unloading scene at Red Lion; the couple in the lobby asked me if they could help. For the next hour, they visited with residents, reassured them and helped set up cots in the banquet room. They then singled me out and handed me a room key. They had paid for a room for staff, realizing that we would need to be able to restore ourselves with naps and showers. This small gesture was huge. Those of us who stayed with the residents "hot bunked" (took turns sleeping in the beds) and were able to sufficiently refresh to survive the next 48 hours.

We re-boarded the vans after 48 hours when we got the "all clear" to return to Heritage Heights. There had been no serious incidents, no residents injured, ill or lost. Their home in Chelan was prepared and ready for their return. In looking back there are many moments that make me shudder, others that me smile and the generosity of that couple consistently warms me with the spirit of goodness. Crises truly do bring out the best in people. The residents rallied and were real soldiers down there in Wenatchee. The staff able to work did so with unforgettable enthusiasm, kindness and awesome reserves of energy. Their teamwork continues to fill me with gratitude. And those two Good Samaritans will remain close to my heart forever as models of whom I hope I can emulate as we go forward. Thank you.

Michelle Jerome - November 10, 2015

EVACUATION EXPERIENCE

So many wild fires have occurred recently
in this part of the state.
All power went out at Heritage Heights on
Friday, August 14ᵗʰ, and all residents had to evacuate.

Early August 15ᵗʰ, I quickly packed a handbag
with a few needed clothes.
Also, I grabbed my zip-lock bag containing
bathroom needs to use wherever
I might go.

My friend, Ruth Keys saw me walking out
carrying several packed bags and invited
me to escape with her and stay at her
daughter's house in Manson.
I agreed, because that change for me would be a time of fun.

Molly, Ruth's daughter, had spoken to the
nurse about my R.X. pills and doses
of eye drops.
Because she would be taking care of me,
I instantly knew what I would later swap.

Most of the other residents had to stay and
sleep in one huge room of the Red Lion
Hotel in Wenatchee.
Because the residents had to sleep on hard
low cots with thin mattresses, I thank
God it was not me.

I stayed during the evacuation time with Bob
and Molly Hoots and had an unfolding
great time.
Even though the electricity was out at least one
and a-half days in Manson, I still felt as
if I was living on cloud nine.

For two nights I slept on the lower mattress of
the grandsons' bunk bed.
Each time I arose or got in, I had to take
care not to bump my head.

Each moment was never dull, but filled with
surprising fun.
Molly and Bob's eleven-month-old toy dog,
when not asleep, was always on the run!
Baxter loved to catch and chase his thrown ball or toys.

On the second morning there, I was fully
dressed, but walked around Molly's
house for a while in my socks.
I finally tried to put my shoes on and
for a moment, was totally shocked.

Both laces of the left shoe were cold and
damp.
While chewing on them, the dog didn't care;
he thought he was a champ.

When the power was out, the foods Molly
served were never cold.

She parked their travel trailer near the back
porch and prepared everything on
it's gas stove.

Monday, August 17th was the day on which
Molly drove her mom and me back to Heritage Heights.
To thank Molly for her loving care during
the time of evacuation, I gave her
one of my first created books to
show my thank-you rights.

By Ann Zion - September 9, 2015

12:00 *Chelan Fire and Rescue when the winds shifted in the afternoon and began threatening the South Chelan Neighborhoods. Responded first to the low income housing at the end of South Bradley Street and began assisting with evacuations and then moved to Rowe's Towing to tell them to evacuate. The fire was fast approaching Rowe's Towing.*
12:37 *Starting Level 2 evacuation in Apple Acres on the west side to Washington Creek*
13:50 *We have fire running down into the city, if they have any additional air support*
13:56 *West Woodin, hot embers falling on the dock and fuel tanks, they are wetting things down but need assistance*
14:00 *There are 3 structures burning on Anderson Road*
14:14 *East Iowa, one structure lost up on the hillside, also multi alarms going off in Jan Rowe's Junk Yard, also we'll need a contingency plan for Chelan Falls, it's heading that way. Crews disengage and retreat to a safe distance from fires; this area had zero visibility from heavy fire and high winds pushing smoke to the ground*
15:22 *Walmart Level 3 Evacuation*
15:25 *Antoine fire blew up approximately. Fire grew quickly to a column dominated fire covering ridge to valley floor to the other ridge.*

HEARTS ON FIRE

It is no secret Lake Chelan is a favored destination for vacationers and adventurers. Thousands of people flock to enjoy all that Lake Chelan offers, particularly in the warm months of summer, when the heat of the sunlight can get up to over a hundred degrees. Fires from the intense heat, winds and lightning have been an expected situation each year. The warning signs are posted and the firefighters are on alert to protect our town when this occurs.

I fell in love with Lake Chelan in the summer that I turned seventeen. I traveled with my two best girlfriends for a fun weekend, arriving from the West side that was constantly rainy and gray. The beauty of the lake, mountains and endless stars in the evenings amazed me. Downtown was small but the township was very quaint. The three of us camped with no tent at the Don Morse Memorial Park. We played in the sun and water by day and slept under the stars at night. As young gals, we had very little money. We ate lettuce and tomato sandwiches all weekend to ration our money for beer. We pooled our funds and treated ourselves to an order of fries from the Lakeview Drive-In. Back then the price, I think, was sixty-five cents. We shared and dipped them in ketchup as we savored them one-by-one. The fries tasted delightful.

There is no place like Lake Chelan to fill your soul, regardless of age from your youth or later in life with well-earned wrinkles. Since that time from my younger self, I have returned to Lake Chelan every year; spreading the word about this little slice of heaven that I had discovered that weekend in Eastern Washington.

The years passed and I raised my family. We then began our traditions of vacations and reunions, enjoying Lake Chelan together. We were not born here or grandfathered in like so many others, but our love for Lake Chelan runs deep and we carry it in our hearts, as if we were natives. I have felt a part of Lake Chelan for almost forty years now. My husband Kelly and I currently call it home, living on the south shore of this majestic lake.

In the summer of 2015, there were raging fires burning all over the Pacific Northwest, including Oregon and Idaho. The previous year there were devastating fires in Pateros, Washington, which almost completely burned the small town down. It is common to have fires in Eastern Washington, being an especially dry climate and high desert terrain. The intense heat of summer, while enjoyable, makes for high-fire warnings. People are aware of that fact, including our defenders, the firefighters. They are prepared and ready. Only this year was different. In the month of August, the safety of family, friends, neighbors, townspeople and many animals were at risk when the Chelan Complex fires began and became out of control. The fires burned wildly in many different locations all at once. These fires caused fear and panic throughout the town, near the town and on the outskirts of town. It appeared everywhere you looked. There was heavy smoke or burning flames, causing homes, properties and businesses to be incinerated to ashes or damaged in some form.

We saw firsthand, large and small areas of our town go up in flames. The surrounding fires burned simultaneously. As my family followed the flames from our home patio, we felt the emotional sadness and stress for ourselves and many others. It scorched us with grief and sorrow in our hearts, knowing these fires left some people homeless, losing all their possessions and deeply scarring them, as they remember the ashes from the final destruction.

The fear and panic created from the Chelan Complex fires came in waves for many people in many forms. One large problem was the outside health hazard. You couldn't breathe the air. The smoke was so heavy you couldn't see through it. Most days you couldn't even see the lake, the smoke was so thick. Our grandchildren viewed the flames with us from our patio. They were so scared. It broke my heart to see the fear in their eyes. They were accustomed to having joy and laughter with Grandma and Grandpa and enjoyed the freedom to not have a care in the world.

My husband works in Wenatchee and drives 97A twice a day. When the cell phone towers near the Knapps Tunnel, burned down, the State Patrol barricaded both routes of travel north and south. It remained closed for endless hours and remained closed for days at a time on other days—no one could make it through. On the Highway, folks sat in their cars watching the increasing backed up line of cars happen and the flames still burning. My husband was like so many others that waited in line anxiously and could not call or get home. With a racing heart and concern for his family's safety, fear overwhelmed him. There was nothing he could do except wait with a helpless feeling in his gut. At home, we worried about his welfare as well—having no communication with anyone. KOZI Radio Station was our only source for information. We were glued to the radio, listening for any and all fire reports or updates. KOZI was our lifeline and they did an amazing job of keeping people informed, particularly during the days when we had no internet or phone lines to rely on.

Being on a Level 3 Evacuation for weeks was intense to say the least. Seeing red, hot embers in our driveway from the high-force winds was beyond our control and created more fear. Not knowing what the night would bring, we were afraid to close our eyes to sleep. The questions on our minds: Would we wake up the next morning or be lucky enough to hear a knock on the door, telling us to evacuate in time? Would the highway be open to get away safely somewhere? Or would we be stung by destruction? Weeks of sleepless nights and pacing occurred during this time. Walking outside or looking out the window you saw the flames burning as wildfires do, across the lake, behind us and to the south side of us. Homes disintegrated from the fires within our few mile radiuses, leaving people with nothing and having to stay with friends or at a shelter.

My son suffered an illness during this time that needed hospital attention. Chelan Hospital is only five miles from our home so my youngest son drove him that afternoon to the ER. Long story short, due to the fires reaching the road on 97A north and the roads being closed, they were not able to come back home until the following morning. The next day the hospital was shut down for a period of time, as they had no power.

My kids ended up having to leave when 97A reopened and the family time had ended. I was relieved my loved ones got home safely and away from the dangerous fires. Kelly and I chose to stick it out and trust God for our safety. Our family and friends disagreed with our choice to stay, and they felt fearful for us for not evacuating.

The fire fighters were unbelievable. They worked day and night trying to save peoples' homes and to contain the fires. Volunteers and firefighters arrived from all over the country to assist and serve our residential area, while the townspeople joined together helping everyone they could in every manner possible.

I did not personally know the people that lost their homes,

but a few of my friends in town did know them. I knew firsthand that they opened their hearts in generosity, giving back to their community. They helped those folks with needed shelter and food.

Life has given us many trials throughout the years. Constantly reminded of the difficult situations we have overcome together, Kelly and I are thankful. Through this frightening experience, our core beliefs remained resilient. We rely on God's direction, kept the daily prayer chains ongoing, held strong in our faith and the honest reality of what is most important in life.

"It's not what we have in our life, but who we have in our life that matters."

In spite of the fire risk each summer, I love living in Chelan. My family and friends will continue to enjoy all that it has to offer and keep on making new memories for many years to come. The rewards of living the Chelan life far outweigh the fear of any flames.

Author Deborah Brodie-Foust

15:29 Anderson Rd has been checked and there is no one there, we will try to figure out where the kids went, it was probably a neighbor getting them out.

15:33 Children found, were taken to the elementary school, no longer need contact

16:48 Advised of possible kids in the Howard Flats Rd residence.

16:49 Responding to Howard Flats Rd. Chelan Falls to a report from RC that there were children possibly still in a residence on Howard Flats Rd that was on fire. Upon arrival at Howard Flats Rd we were unable to access the address due to heavy fire across road. Went in via Apple Acres to try and access from the north on Howard Flats Rd. While in route, it was reported they had made contact with someone and confirmed there were no children in house at reported address. Responded back to Chelan Falls area to make further assessment of resource needs as fire approached.

She came uninvited and unwelcomed, but as intrusive as she always is she pushed herself into our lives early in the morning on August 14, 2015. She arrived with a "flashing, striking blow" followed by an earthshaking clap of thunder—starting up a week of terror and fright. With her forceful ways she threatened the safety of our home causing emotions to run high and putting stress on a plain of its own. She started in her own small way as always, but with no immediate intervention she grew in velocity, power and strength. There then became concern for action involving machines and manpower. Like a never-ending ocean wave she grew from a very small extinguishable trespasser to consuming over 600,000 acres of forest, fields, homes, meadows, hills and mountains. She was a "beast" with fire lapping at all she come in contact with. Burning, destroying, killing and maiming was her aim for fame. She ruined, depressed, saddened, chased, unraveled and left homeless those that she chose to attack. To escape her fiery temper was only through a change of direction in the wind, a blessing from God, strength and determination of the fearless fire fighters putting their lives on the line for others, or if you believe in luck, that's what you were, LUCKY, VERY LUCKY!

Help **FINALLY ARRIVED!** Helicopters with hanging water buckets and long elephant-like noses scooped and sucked up water which was wonderfully accessible to them from beautiful Lake Chelan. Awe...water so close at hand, liquid gold! A priceless liquid to help quench the ever growing flames. A tool so close at hand and a saving factor in such a desperate situation. C1-30 bombers loaded with borate retardant and large DC-10 twin engine scooper air tankers, with bellies that held 1,100 gals of water upon skimming the surface of the lake, came on the scene to help defend us and fight this wicked and fiery monster. Flames raging and suffocating black smoke filled the air with harmful and deadly fumes. Horror filled our minds as we watched the flames crawl closer and closer to the hill just behind our home.

As an occasional deterrent our eyes would focus upward on an awesome, yet frightening, air show that would descend over our house not 30 feet in the air. Like angels from heaven they came out of nowhere to assist in the battle that they were assigned to win. Three planes determined to fight the "beast," that was raging out of control, did their maneuvers with skill and exactness. A small guide plane led the way directing the bombers that were determined to make their efforts count.

A good downpour would have been like manna from the heaven, but to our dismay the wind in all its gusto began to blow. Fueling the now huge flames the wind was doing, as we have heard before, "Adding fuel to the fire!" The fire continued to rage hotter and hotter and to move faster and faster sending families from their homes to shelters and evacuation levels rising from 1 to 2 to 3! Run, run, run! Some only made it with their lives and left EVERYTHING behind to be devoured by this fiery beast. A level 3 was our status as we beheld the flames creeping over the top of the hill behind our home.

Bushes, bushes, so many bushes, they must be cut down! Fifteen arborvitae bushes, some 40 plus years old, so quickly cut to the ground, but too close to the house to leave as an invitation for the hot embers to settle into and explode with intentions of engulfing our home in flames and then into utter ablation. Such a small sacrifice to, perhaps, save our home. Sprinkler on the roof, lawn and bushes kept wet, valuables hurriedly collected and loaded into car, mind racing, planes roaring, panic in the air, inhaling smoke, tourist hurriedly rushing to leave town, roads blocked, people frantic for the safety of their lives, their belongings and their beloved animals, but first and far most the safety of loved ones.

Two homes that stand alone on the hill, the hill that the fire is advancing down, are enveloped with smoke, are they still there? A spray of foam from brave fire fighters has rescued and saved these dwellings. What a grand sight to see as the smoke moves on, and we get a glance of those homes still in tack.

The flames continue to creep toward our home and the homes next to us. My mind is in a state of shock. Such a surreal picture unfolding before our eyes. As the flames reach to within 50 yards of the dirt road next to our property two loads of borate are dropped along the ever advancing line of fire. I wanted to hug the pilot of that plane, for his efforts killed the monster that we so dreaded, the monster that was advancing towards us with the intent to destroy. The high winds were giving more threat to devastation. As they changed direction heading east it became evident that we were most likely out of danger, but the threat of destruction didn't end with us. No, the fire roared on and on and on until it had devoured homes, apple packing and storage sheds and businesses. There was no rhyme or reason for how it proceeded on its destructive journey.

Power poles had burned cutting power to hundreds of homes and businesses, but work was begun immediately for restoration of this power. As evening fell the town was veiled in darkness. PUD workers
pushed forward in their quest to bring "light" back into our lives. New power poles and wires were installed in a hurried but efficient fashion giving us unprecedented respect for those responsible in replacing such
an essential luxury. Within forty-eight-hours power had resumed making many thankful for the miracle of electricity.

The fire moved on bringing horror to others along its way.

We have moved on with our lives. There are reminders all around us of the fury that interrupted our lives that morning of August 14, 2015. We are grateful that our home and that our lives were spared. This experience has changed our lives and we are living the "happy ending."

As a note: My emotions ran especially high during this summer of heavy fires, the worst in Washington State History, because we have two beloved grandsons, Carter and Bennet Murch that are brothers, working and fighting these fires. They have been safe, and I pray that they and all those who are involved in fighting these fires will continue to be kept safe. Bless them all!

Written by: Susan Yanac
8-14-15

Fire—A Different Point of View

Fire. I've always been intrigued by fire. When I was a kid, I loved to help burn brush on our farm, throwing sticks and small branches onto the bonfire and feeling the heat on my face. I loved the way the flames danced and twirled in a myriad of colors, loved the smell of the burning fir branches, and loved the crackling sound the fire made. I once found a hole burned in a ribbon that had been tied around my pony tail while we worked, but I always felt safe. My dad was in charge and he was the smartest man on Earth. He knew what he was doing.

Almost every year, my dad's logging crew was sent to places around the state to fight fires. I wonder now if he ever fought fires around Chelan. I would ask my mom when he would be coming home, and she would always say, "When their work's finished and the fire's out." When he was gone for more than a couple of days, I would start to worry about him. *Is he safe? How much danger is he in? Will he make it home okay? What is taking so long?*

Eventually, he would return, exhausted and dirty and ready for a bath, a home-cooked meal, and a good night's sleep. He would tell us where he had been fighting fires, but the names were unfamiliar to me. Today, I wonder if logging crews are still sent to fight fires, and I wonder how many little girls and boys are stuck at home worrying about their dads and moms who are out there risking their lives.

I'm still intrigued by fire, but now I understand how very dangerous it is; how it can destroy, kill and how it can change people forever. I was saddened this year when the Wolverine fire started and grew bigger. I was concerned for the people who had to be evacuated and those who lost animals. Our beautiful Chelan filled with smoke, and I was starting to cough. It was a relief that we had a trip planned to fly to Dallas, Texas, to celebrate our granddaughter's second birthday and to care for her while her parents worked. We had three weeks of fun ahead and wouldn't be breathing smoke.

We had barely started our vacation when our daughter in Chelan called to tell us that another fire had started from a lightning strike. It was growing swiftly and threatening Chelan. After she rescued her kids from their dad's house, as the fire raged dangerously close, she assured us that she and her family were safe.

Immediately, Bill and I started watching Facebook for updates. The fires kept growing. We saw that people were being evacuated. We saw that one of the fires was only a few blocks from our house. The fires kept growing. We started worrying about people we know. Would they have homes to return to? We were over 2000 miles away and there was nothing we could do, except pray. So we prayed. We watched the news. We kept looking at Facebook. The fires kept growing. We heard that many people had lost their homes and lots more were in danger of losing theirs. We read that Jon and Robie Luke had lost their home and the shop where we had recently taken our dog, Maggie, for her first set of dog training. The fires kept growing. It seemed that they were joining together. The pictures on Facebook were ghastly. The whole town was filled with heavy smoke. Would there still be a Chelan when we returned?

When it was time to come home, we felt much trepidation. Would we even recognize Chelan? The images in our minds were pictures of blackened devastation. We nervously drove through the tunnel and then searched the sky for smoke, but it seemed pretty clear. As we drove closer, we started seeing the burn line on the hills and saw the blackened Butte. And then Lake Chelan came into view. It was beautiful. It was clean. The air was clear. The sky was blue. The land around the lake was green. There were still fires burning around the area, but Chelan has survived.

As I think back to how exhausted my dad was when he returned from fighting fires for a few days, I think about the fire fighters who have been working for weeks to put out our fires, risking their lives so we can have homes and a town to live in. I wonder if they have any idea how much we appreciate them. They are heroes, although I suspect that they wouldn't consider themselves such. I thank God for them. My heart is filled to bursting with love, pride and gratitude for each one of them!

Linda Crego - September 2015

TO OUR FRIENDS AND FAMILY

I am using this technology to get word to you about our situation here in Chelan. Many of you have reached out asking if we are ok and in most cases I've sent a brief response stating I would send more information later. Today is Tuesday August 18, 2015, 10:00 am. We again have power, cell phone service, and local radio station, KOZI is back on the air giving us updates. I now have a bit of time to give you that promised information. As I write this one of the enormous fire-fighting helicopters just flew low over our smoky back yard reminding me that the fire fight continues. There are still people in need and others who are exhausted but still working to save homes and protect and assist others. The smoke is still thick. I can barely see the outline of the burned Butte not far away. Here is my statement about our recent experiences:

I can't believe it's been just four days since last Friday, August 14 when about 4:45 am there was a very loud clap of thunder. Jim was already up but the thunder woke me. We went out to our back yard pool area where it appeared to be another hot sunny day in Chelan. Because of the thunder we thought we would get rain so we began moving cushions and other things under cover. We both happened to look to the Butte, a large hill and the view from the front of our house. We saw two small fires begin to burn on the Butte clearly the result of lightning strikes. We immediately called 911 though we were not the first to call. For the next hour or so we watched the two fires. The one on the left had started as a perfect circle; the one on the right began as a rectangle. The fires spread but then appeared to be out...clearly this was not the case! As time passed the fires spread until a good part of the Butte was involved.

The rest of Friday and then Saturday seem like weeks!! Fire was everywhere! In every direction from our house we could see flames on the hills. We became a war zone with planes and helicopters grabbing water from the lake and dumping on the fires. There was a big passenger plane, a DC 10 dumping red fire retardant. The firefight was happening on the hills but also in business and residential areas of our little town of Chelan. Every run of the planes and helicopters went directly over our house! Wop, wop, wop of the enormous helicopters! Planes flying so low one could almost count the rivets on their belly.

My daughter, Kristi and her family including husband, Tony, their three children and three more kids ages 10 through 16 were visiting Chelan and staying at their little vacation home not far from us but across the Lake and the Chelan River. They are located at the base of the Butte about a block from the High school. They are within walking distance of our house. Soon their neighborhood was at a level 3 evacuation. The kids were already in the pool at our place so Kristi and Tony loaded up their two vehicles and came to our place too.

We have just finished building a pool and a pool house with outdoor kitchen, bathroom, and guest sleeping space. This was really the first time we have had so many guests at once and it proved to be a godsend. Though there was all the fire-fighting activity the kids were in the pool, we had food, we had, for a while, electricity, so we had a party! It's hard to believe but it was still Friday! Then power went out, Internet and cable went out, some cell service stopped. The smoke was thick. It became obvious that the situation was getting so much worse! Kristi and Tony elected to load up kids and all their gear and leave town, returning to Bellingham Friday evening. It was a good decision.

Jim and I have stayed. We were without power for 36 hours. Our Verizon cell service eventually went out. On Friday our local radio station, KOZI, lost its ability to broadcast. On Monday all services returned.

Fires and evacuations continue in surrounding areas on both sides of the lake but the town itself is in clean-up mode. There have been homes and businesses burned. One can see streets, homes, and vehicles covered with the red flame retardant. Many roads, streets, and businesses remain closed. The fires still rage in canyons and wooded areas. There are still homes and other structures in danger. Kristi and Tony's home is fine. The smoke is still here and will be

58

for some time.

One other thing: Jim uses a C-Pap machine so had a rough night on Friday with no power. He had to sleep sitting up in his chair. When we still had no power on Saturday we made arrangements to stay the night with our building contractor in Orondo where there was power. Reid and Sandy were welcoming and such gracious hosts. There was another guest as well, a young woman unable to return to her home in Pateros. We had a lovely evening of food and entertainment. Reid called it a shelter party.

Upon returning to our Chelan home Sunday morning, we were greeted with flooded floors in our house. The hot water tank had ruptured! Fortunately, a water damage company was available and the power was on. We now are living in the pool house and the main house is full of big fans --- the adventure continues! We have a comfy bed, kitchen, and bathroom. We have power, cell, cable, and Internet service, we are well, our cats are fine, Bellingham family is fine. Life is good. Karen

15:41 Advising pallets fully involved with fire at Trout Blue Chelan

15:42 Enroute to Rowe's Towing to assist fire.

15:43 Can we get a little more blocked off at SR97A, the fire is coming over the hill and we still have traffic coming down.

15:44 Requested Law Enforcement to expedite.

15:45 Wilmorth Rd on PA giving notifications, the fire is really moving.

15:45 Heli-tanker 736 came in and made a couple of drops south of the houses. Fire picked up while he was doing fuel cycle.

15:48 Wilmorth has multiple spot fires.

15:48 Wilmorth Rd shut down at SR97A

Crews were requested to other areas and deployed. Face-to-face with 503 to check his needs. 503 did not have any needs for me at the high school. An unconfirmed report of fire behind Greens Petroleum was reported and fire moving up the Gorge threatening the structures along Clifford St and Chestnut St. Crews responding.

15:49 Enroute to Walmart, have them close it down completely.

15:50 Released the Okanogan/Douglas County Fire District resources to return to their district with high threat to Alto Lake through Quiet Valley.

A PASSAGE THROUGH FLAMES
By Kent Getzin

CherylAnn and I were awakened early Friday morning, August 14, 2015, at about 4:30AM by a very noisy thunderstorm. I remember thinking, *Crap...just what we need is lightning.* Our house is located on the hillside directly across Lake Chelan from the Chelan Butte, so as I left for work, I saw that the Butte was on fire. Not a large area at that time, but still an active and expanding fire. My thoughts, *Shit...look at that...figures...grrr... just what we need is more smoke in the valley."*

I climbed aboard my motorcycle (referred to as "The Tiger" from here on out) and left for work in Wenatchee, without really thinking much more about it. At about 3:00PM, CherylAnn called me to say her kid's dad and a family friend's homes were threatened by the fire and were on Level 3 Evacuation status. She said she had just spent the last couple of hours helping them evacuate and then helped protect the friend, Miguel's, house by spraying water on the house and shrubs until finally, a huge DC10 flew over and dumped retardant on the area.

At this point, I realized that this fire was serious business and I needed to get home. I immediately left work and went to pick up my thirteen-year-old son, Braden, and headed to Chelan. As I picked up Braden, the wind was blowing pretty vigorously, and I was concerned about weather reports of dust storms predicted for later in the afternoon. After my conversation with CherylAnn, assumptions were made that 97A was likely to close due to the fire, if it had not already closed. Armed with these little bits of incomplete information, I decided it would be best to take the Highway 97 route and enter Chelan via Beebe Bridge at Chelan Falls.

It isn't all that fun riding a motorcycle in windy conditions. Having experienced many rides in windstorms before, you realize you will likely not be blown off the road, but still, you can't account for the actions of others, so I was cautious. When we got to Beebe Bridge, we realized the gravity of the situation. Unable to turn at Chelan Falls due to a roadblock, we decided to forge ahead and take the cut-off into Chelan a few miles ahead.

A mile or so from the bridge we were blown away at all the spot fires on both sides of the road. We began to get nervous. At one point, the fires were within a couple hundred feet of the road, close enough to feel the heat from the nearby blazes. When we arrived at the junction to head east into Chelan, we were faced with another Law Enforcement roadblock. Now, the only alternative was to turn around and go back to Wenatchee via Beebe Bridge or try Apple Acres Road a few miles north of the junction to Chelan.

On toward Apple Acres we went. As we continued on that route, it seemed as though this was a good decision, as no fires or smoke were present. As we approached the intersection of Apple Acres Road and Hwy 97A, next to the Chelan airport, the situation changed and several cars were held up at another roadblock. We stopped and watched as an Officer was casually standing around near the intersection a few feet from his car.

As we sat there calculating our next move, probably not more than a minute or so, we noticed that a dense column of smoke was coming up directly behind the police car. First, I noticed that the police officer was gone. I assume he saw what was about to happen and got into his car. I said to Braden, "Look at all that smoke! It looks like the fire is right below the road." Just then, the wall of smoke burst into flames as the fire crested the top of the hill.

I immediately took off around the cars ahead of me and through the intersection, heading back toward the junction. Now I was starting to panic. *Which way will we go now? We have only a couple options: head north on 97 toward Pateros and wait it out or go back to Beebe Bridge and then back to Wenatchee and try our luck with 97A.* We got a couple hundred yards down the road when we were faced with a large clump of sagebrush on fire on the hillside right next to the road. I slowed to a stop as the winds were fanning the flames and smoke across the road in front of us.

As we sat there, a helicopter with a water bucket was approaching overhead and dropped his quenching payload on the exact spot that we were concerned with. He nailed it, so I took off through the steam, smoke and water of the heli-drop. Arriving at the intersection once again, we decided to try our luck going north toward Pateros. At this point, my cell phone was dead and

Braden's little flip phone had limited service. Wanting to take pictures of our experience, I pulled over to get out my DSLR, which I had in my backpack, only to realize I had left it at my apartment in Wenatchee.

We got back on the Tiger to head to Pateros, only to be stopped in a few hundred feet by dense smoke and fire crossing the highway. I turned around again, thinking our only option left was to head back to Wenatchee via Beebe Bridge. I knew the fires were on both sides of the road and were threatening to cross any moment as we passed through that area only 30 minutes previous, so I wasn't feeling very good about our ability to get back to the bridge. Then of course, a mile or so down HWY 97 toward the bridge, we encountered what looked like a river of dense smoke and fire blowing violently across the road.

At this point, both Braden and I were panicking—we literally had no place left to go. We were trapped by fire in all directions. Our only option was to return to the 97A/Apple Acres Road roadblock and seek assistance from the Sheriff that manned the intersection.

I pulled up and told him in the least panicky voice I could muster (which I am sure was not convincing) that I didn't know what to do. We tried every direction and were surrounded by fire. He very calmly said you can stay here with me. You will be safe here. I am not sure how he figured that, since where we stood was the only place NOT on fire. Flames were all around us and I could not compute how staying there was going to be safe for more than a few minutes. The fires were literally within what seemed like 50 to 100 yards of us on all sides.

Braden was coming unhinged. The Officer was so kind and compassionate with us. He told Braden that he was safe there and that he and I would protect him and that he should try not to worry. He offered for us to sit in his car as we were trying to call CherylAnn, who had no idea of the predicament that we were in. As we sat in his car, he offered us water as we tried multiple times to get through to CherylAnn on Braden's crappy little flip phone. Being a longtime Smart Phone owner, I couldn't figure out how to use the damn thing, so Braden had to keep it together well enough to operate the phone, which had limited service, at best.

We got a few text messages off and only connected long enough with a momentary voice call before getting disconnected, to scare the shit out of CherylAnn. Our garbled and broken attempts at describing our dire circumstances, "We are surrounded by fire!"

After about five minutes, I couldn't stand to sit in the police car any longer and got out. The Officer told me that he had word from some firefighters who had just come from Beebe Bridge that there were occasional breaks in the fire rivers that were crossing the road and that our best bet would be to try to get back to the bridge and to Wenatchee. The fire was worse and crossing the road in several places on the short stretch leading into Chelan. As I was processing what he said we should do, I looked at Braden, who at this point was saying with his eyes, "Did he really just say what I think he said?" I said, "OK, I guess that is the only option." The Sheriff said when we get to places where the fire rivers were crossing the road, wait until it looks like it is "lightening up" then go for it!

We reluctantly got back on the Tiger and headed toward the bridge. As we rode for the first fire crossing, I told Braden that worst case, we could ride into the middle of an orchard and wait it out. He said he thought of the same thing and calmed down a bit.

We approached the first fire crossing, so I slowed down and inched toward the river of smoke cautiously. As we got within twenty or thirty yards of the flow, I said to Braden, "Can you see through it, because I think I can." He confirmed that he thought it looked like it wasn't very wide, so I said, "Ok, let's go for it. Take a deep breath!" I took off, speeding into the dense brown flow. Visibility inside the smoke river was nearly zero and we were being pelted by pieces of what had to be burnt or burning plant matter. As we had hoped, the first "crossing" was probably only 50 to 100 yards across.

I have no idea really how long it took, but we were cheering as we came out the other side. There was one other significant fire river crossing before the Beebe Bridge and safety was before us.

We gratefully rode back to Wenatchee contemplating our experience.

SIXTY-ONE DAYS

Surreal
Red moons descend
Dense grey skies obscure sight
Blood-orange suns awaken

Grateful
Wingless metal thump
Mid-air vessels fill
Smothering uncontrollable rage

Surrounded
Old-growth blazes
Gray matter seeps in, on, over and under
Structures and spirits collapse

Graceful
Ruby-red suppressant spreads relief
Dotted pink houses saved
Towering flames unwillingly surrender

Aggravated
Illusive fresh air strangles the lungs
Displacement, loss and death
Emotions circle around respect and gratitude

Uncertainty
Peaked edges char under yellow moons
Skies crowd with heavy clouds
Black ash trills downward mucking the living

Normalcy
Constellations unveil a brilliant, white full moon
Winds carry burnt mountain dew
Again, windows close tightly

Surreal
Rising honey-amber sun restores faith
Tensions wash away
Evening rains bath memories in reprieve

Written by C. Marchi
October 2015

NOT TO BE FORGOTTEN

Horses, livestock, eagles, bears, hawks, raccoons, farm animals, deer, coyotes, squirrels, wild rabbits and pets unable to evade the fires.

ON CHOOSING YOUR EVACUATION PARTNERS CAREFULLY

So, consider this survival 101: KNOW your survival partners!

I wake in morning, the faithful dog & I. We go out to do our morning watering only to see the fire on the Butte just beginning. The 911 operator tells me "they're on it, thanks for your call". I foolishly assume I can continue my short trip to Wenatchee and all is well. Yeah, lesson 1. never do that! I come back a few short hours later to find my beautiful town surrounded in flames, dense with thick, heavy choking smoke. Not looking good so far.

I frantically procured every survival item imaginable for my dog and me. I grabbed the meal bars, the flashlights & extra batteries. Got the battery powered TV/radio and zip-locked "everything." Dog food for at least 2 weeks. And yes, my hillbilly weapon. I packed the rain gear, plastic bags, flotation devices and, I confess...one designer suit...You know...just in case the media shows up and I might need to look cool. I wish I could say I was kidding, but I can't tell a lie.

As things progress for the worse, dog & I head down to the bluff that looks over the river to the Butte to assess our next move. We pull to the edge and just look out, almost in shock. Two other cars pull up on either side...not close. Some get out, but all just stare ahead at the flaming mountain so very close, watching the embers blow our way. No one says a word. It's like "doomsday" movies we've all seen. A cold silence. It's 90 degrees, but cold inside your body. One by one, we just drive away. Neighbors who all know each other, but nothing is said.

Suddenly, the word is out: All roads out are blocked with fire, no way out except into the Lake..."if" it comes to that. I'm hitching up the boat to my truck just in case. Dog & I run back to check on our shared home, to find, in my great dismay, that no one else is packed! Mind you, the fire is burning strong just over a block away and our neighbors are all evacuating. I take it upon myself to gently

ask of my sweetest & dearest of friends, "Hey, have you thought about packing? We may need to go!"
She says, "Hmmmmm, you're right. I should get some things together."

I feel so much better now, knowing she is taking this dangerous situation really seriously.
Dog & I head back out to Manson to check on my elderly parents. There are no phones, and now, no electricity. They are in good hands with the generator shared with the neighbors so we're feeling good...Dog & I—back home we go!

Nearly a ghost town as we drive though. Everyone looking out for their own. I pull up to the house with my evacuation plans replaying over & over in my head. Once again, TO MY DISMAY, I enter the home.... there is my sweetest & dearest of friends, with every type of tote bag known to man! From Seahawks to Bloomingdales, packed, overflowing, blocking the entire foyer......yep, she's packed!

I look from bag to bag only to find family photos, china, candle holders, Waterford crystal & God only knows what else! I'm looking...looking...don't see any clothing, food or any remote resemblance of survival gear...What on earth?

Here comes my "sweetest & dearest of friends" with yet another tote of crap! I ask her, "My friend, are your clothes or personal items packed somewhere? I don't know...maybe a little food?" She replies "Hmmm...I hadn't thought of that, I guess I should get a change of clothes & a toothbrush." Apparently, she was planning to go on holiday at a gallery!

So I say to my "sweetest & dearest of friends,"I say, "So, if we are forced to float in the lake to survive...What exactly are you bringing to the table?" While we are all sharing our snack bars & toilet paper...what exactly will you have to offer? Do you think we will all be so entertained by your family photos that we will forget we are hungry, wet and cold? Will we eat our crackers off our fine china? I think not! I think you will be the first one thrown over when the snack bars get low! God forbid we would be there very long...lest

69

you would be the first one eaten!"

My sweetest and dearest of friend says "Hmmmm, I hadn't thought about that". But in true & consistent form, she then has the audacity to ask, "Hey, if we do have to leave, could you please grab my grandmothers' framed button collections?" (REALLY? Seriously, REALLY!?) "And maybe that large painting on the wall?" Like if I have room for anything else in my truck......which I don't, I'm going to put her grandmothers' freaking button collection before my 48" TV! Not a chance!

All I can say is you may want to plan ahead for your next emergency. And, definitely scout your survival partners in advance. Personally, I'm going over today to talk to the neighbors to see what they have going on. Choose well my friend, it could mean your very survival. You may need to "pack" for some of your special loved ones.

Though a very slight shift in the wind could have changed our lives forever, the good news is we still have this beautiful home. But more importantly, she is still my sweetest & dearest of friend!

Foot note: We did not have to go into the lake, but my next survival adventure will not include my sweetest and dearest of friends.

Written by Shelly Finnigan Ward

15:50 *Received instructions to head to the warehouse area. It took a bit to get a feel for what was happening. The smoke was thick and fire was pressing on several structures—two or three warehouses were fully involved. Additional resources arrived including a brush truck from Okanogan and Douglas County. Advised that there was a 10,000-gallon tank of anhydrous ammonia so crew was withdrawn, a representative from Chelan Fruit advised that it was propane. Re-engaged crew. About this time the lumber yard lit up. An additional warehouse lit up. We received a tower from Ephrata and an engine from Grant County. Wilbur Ellis just began to burn. At this point we were trying to simply protect exposure. Attempted to protect the RV's at the storage lot. We noticed a compromised power pole. Crew withdrew and the pole fell where they were parked. A strange guy walked up and stated he was walking through. I advised him not to. In his shorts and tank top he headed off into the firestorm. I do not know what happened to him. I heard he jumped in a car shortly after walking into the smoke. All of the trailers lit up one by one. We lost water and began working on a solution. We were without water for about two or three hours. Fire truck caught fire due to the engine intake sucking in large amounts of embers. They were able to put it out, limped it to town and were flagged down by Les Schwab employees who informed them it was on fire again while they were driving it. Les Schwab ran and grabbed several extinguishers (7) and put the truck fire out. Wilbur Ellis unable to be fully extinguished before we lost water. Meanwhile, the ladder trucks sat and crews worked to move product from the unaffected building at Chelan Fruit. A pile of pallets lit up next to the unaffected building—used tank water* and had a few trucks shuttle water in from Walmart though able to get it knocked out. Once we had water again, we knocked embers out of the smoke and protected two buildings that survived. Ephrata was able to continue to knock down and mop up the Wilbur Ellis fire. Limited on what could be accomplished with the warehouse fires due to resources, water and high wind forcing us to bed ladders; stayed on this fire for the night. Opinion: if pallets and bins were not stored so close to the warehouses, the buildings would have survived. Safety dialogue ensued.

WAKE-UP CALL
Written by Mary Epperson

Six friends had arrived from Seattle on Thursday to stay a week at Wapato Point Resort. An electrical storm started after everyone had gone to bed. The thunder was so loud that our friends awoke to the shaking of their condo.

The next day, the Butte fire burned fields, homes, businesses, power poles and one transformer station—cutting off power for all of Chelan and Manson. It was out for 36 hours.

The first thing the Wapato Point Resort staff did, once the power went out, was to knock on all the guests' doors, advising them not to flush the toilets. Without power, the sewage couldn't be pumped out to the main line from the holding tanks. One of our friends overheard a mother with an infant and a two-year-old say, "How am I going to do that?" The Wapato Point staff told the guests, "Power might not be restored for two weeks."

Saturday morning brought backed up toilets and pools of sewage in the open grassy play field on the resort. Guests couldn't cook, except on barbeques, nor turn on lights, use their cell phones, nor keep their fresh food safely cold. There was a major exodus from Wapato Point Resort and every other hotel in the area.

At our house, we had candles, flashlights and a generator that powered freezers and a refrigerator. I'd prepared for dinner guests the day before, and dinner was served at our home. My only inconvenience that evening was to cook the crab macaroni and cheese and the peach crisp on the barbeque. It was actually kind of fun. I felt like I was camping as we sat around illuminated by candlelight discussing the fire and the poor emergency preparedness from the Wapato Point Resort staff.

The fires were a wake-up call for everyone. Our friends drove over to the Red Apple Market in Manson to buy ice to keep their food cold. They had a cooler. Between the 6 of them, they had only $3.00 in cash. Few others couldn't purchase much either, since the credit card system was dead without power. No one thought of carrying much cash while on vacation.

Our friends had purchased one bag of ice. Luckily for them, they could bring the bulk of their food over to our house to keep it cold. The power went back on at 1:30AM Sunday in downtown

Manson. By that time, only 20% of the Wapato Point Resort guests remained.

This unexpected example of life without power, however brief, affected more than just the guests at Wapato Point. While driving back to Manson from a trip to Wenatchee, I found myself reflecting on the stores, shops, wineries and restaurants that had to dispose of their food because it had spoiled during those 36 hours without refrigeration.

Ten days later, we drove south to Wenatchee. Leaving the smoke-filled valley of Chelan was a bonus for our breathing and it highlighted the difference between the two areas. Wenatchee had some smoke, but you could still see the hills.

By now, Chelan looked like those old photos of Eastern Washington towns after Mount Saint Helens exploded. The few people walking the downtown of Chelan appeared like shadow figures. Everything looked grey because it was covered with a thin film of ash. The lake was so filled with smoke you couldn't see past the edge. There was no sun, only a red ball in the sky.

During our drive back from Wenatchee to Manson, just 45 minutes, the temperature dropped 17 degrees, from 89-72 degrees.

Chelan City Park, usually packed in August with campers, only contained local residents living in RV's. Most of these people had been ordered to evacuate from their property because their homes were in danger of being destroyed.

The Chelan Valley was surrounded by wild fires. Ash was visibly falling within the smoke, the results of the ongoing fires. You couldn't tell which fire was raging: First Creek, Chelan Complex, or the Wolverine Fire. Being outside was like standing *in* a campfire.

I'd been researching a way to drive to Banff, Alberta, B.C. without running into smoke at the end of August for a previously scheduled trip. I'd been looking at the Western State Incident Fire Report sites hoping to discover a smoke-free route. The fires were everywhere. We would've had to travel 500 miles, through British Columbia, Eastern Washington, Idaho, Montana and the Western parts of Alberta, all of which had fires. I pictured a continuous smoky sky as we headed east and then north toward Banff. The mental picture reminded me of an old prophecy that I'd read, *The West would be covered in fire.*

Well, here it is.

74

16:07 *Shut down SR97 at the BeeBe Bridge*

16:08 *Fire above Apple Acres Road above the RV Park.*

16:08 *Assembling at engine and a tender for warehouse fires.*

16:12 *Fire on ridge near Apple Acres R, ½ - ¾ miles from residences.*

16:12 *Enroute to Chelan Falls.*

16:14 *Fire is cresting the hill near Chelan Falls ½ mile from residences and where subjects will be able to evacuate.*

16:14 *SR97A, fire below the airport, spreading north, going fast.*

16:20 *Jumped into town; crossed river & running; joining spot across (100 acres) Columbia River and working E&N; burning multi structures and threatened; winds making rotors have to sit down.*

16:20 *Chelan Falls area to close the highway, fire on both sides of the roadway. See if any units can head that way to close it down.*

Upon arrival at BeeBe Bridge, we encountered heavy traffic and detours due to fire conditions, downed power lines at Chelan Falls and evacuation traffic.

16:29 *SR97A, fire moving towards residence, is about 40 feet away. Reporting Party not evacuating area, wetting down with hose.*

16:30 *Howard Flats Rd, fire coming up hill toward back of the houses.*

16:31 *Six fires on the other side of the Columbia River where the new construction is. Diverted to McNeil Canyon to address spotting and structure protection issues. Made contact with Chief on the corner of Wilmorth and SR97 and was briefed to current situation (much fire/little resources). Was able to ascertain some of the units in the vicinity but many were unidentified.*

16:33 *Report of a house on fire at the airport, Howard Flats Road.*

16:35 *Phones are down.*

16:35 Unknown fire unit called saying they are out of resources and want Kittitas County called.

16:35 Residence at Apple Acres Road refusing to leave. There are three people in side, can't get out due to smoke.

16:36 Level 3 Evacuation at Apple Acres Trailer Park.

16:36 Spot fires all the way down SR97A and SR97, structures threatened, fire within 50-150 feet from residences.

16:38 Howard Flats RD, unknown if all occupants are out of the house.

16:39 Caller says he knows people are inside, unknown how many.

16:42 At SR97A and SR97 one structure threatened.

16:42 Reporting party said there's children in the house.

16:43 Ephrata Fire advised Grant County Strike Team, two engines and a ladder coming up from HWY 7, over the BeeBe Bridge.

BECAUSE YOU ALWAYS LISTEN TO ME

I sent this to good friends just to share with them some thoughts and feelings I was experiencing. It was an emotional time for me.

Memories, observations, emotions: here are some things I want to write down so I can pull up the memories in the future:

How fast it all happens! Friday, Aug 14, 2015 started for me at 4:45 am and I went to bed about 10:00 p.m. It feels like weeks!!

Jim was "sleeping" in his chair. He could not lie down because he would stop breathing. I was so disappointed that the Red Cross had moved out of town...we needed them! They had moved to Entiat, too far away and it's unknown whether roads were closed—very disappointing.

Friday night dark and quiet: I'm a person who loves quietness. Quietness is hard to find...there are sounds of TV, radio, vehicles, machines, heating or cooling, yes even fire-fighting planes and helicopters. But Friday night August 15, 2015, in Chelan, WA, it was quiet...I hesitate to say dead quiet but the quietness was lovely! And, it was dark! There was no electric power in the entire community so we had total darkness. The darkness allowed us to see the hundreds, perhaps thousands, of fires still burning on the Butte. During daylight the Butte looked completely black, totally burned. However, the darkness showed us the fires still burning there. I could also see fires burning on the ridges behind our house to the southeast. However, on our little Allen Ave in Chelan and everywhere nearby it was dark! I took a little walk alone, not far but far enough to know I was surrounded by quiet darkness. It was strangely peaceful. I found this sensory deprivation to be calming and very pleasant. It felt like a gift, selfish I know given what others were experiencing but I took it as a personal gift. While Jim had to struggle to sleep and breathe simultaneously, I spent the night in deep natural sleep with no sounds and no light. Selfishly glorious!

The power went out! Yikes! Why had I not considered the possibility of losing power? While we had two good working flashlights we had others that didn't work and no extra batteries. Tony and Kristi were still here and I decided I needed to get batteries if at all possible. I went to the Safeway store about 1/2 block away and they were open! The store was totally dark except for the cashiers running the tills using generators...they even took debit and credit cards! I bought batteries and ice. The Safeway employees were pleasant, calm, in good humor as were all customers I saw. No one was in a panic, we were all orderly chatting among ourselves, getting to know neighbors, people had to use cell phones or flashlights to find what they needed on the dark shelves but we were grateful Safeway was there. Saturday morning, I went to Safeway hoping for a newspaper and ice. They weren't open yet...they had to clean up spoiling food, so I didn't get a newspaper but an employee at the ice freezer outside was willing to sell me two bags of ice, $1.00 each.

WRITTEN BY KAREN CLARK

17:03 *Relaying to PUD that substation near end of airport on Howard Flats Road is threatened, concern is if it goes we will hose water pressure.*

17:06 *There are two juveniles and one elderly male at Apple Acres Road that need a ride out. Enroute to get them out.*

17:06 *SR97 saying the fire is about a football field from the residence and "get your F***ing A**es here now.*

Responded to a RC report of a residents at SR97 were frantic and told RC they had fire a 100 ft from their house and were trapped.

17:07 *Two people out of a burning residence and there and there is still one subject inside. Unknown exact address, west of SR97/SR97A.*

17:09 *Yakima County not available to send any resources.*

17:13 *Fire that took out the junk yard, jumped over East Iowa, working its way through the dry grass where the PUD Gorge trail is.*

17:17 *Green Petroleum is afraid fire is going to get to the industrial site on SR150.*

17:19 *Fire is coming up the Gorge on Cemetery Road.*

17:24 *PUD power to Chelan Fruit has tripped open, it is de-energized*

17:26 *Cemetery Road, multiple structures going up*

17:28 *Stove oil, diesel oil, gasoline, maybe aviation fuel. Reporting party is not on scene. Fire is below the plant now. Thinks it's coming back up and there's another fire coming from the side. Reporting party advised Fire Chief contacted the plant and told them to evacuate already. Reporting party is afraid the oil could be spilled in the Columbia River too.*

FIRE ON THE BUTTE

It was almost getting up time. I was lying in bed with my eyes closed, listening to the approaching storm. I felt a flash in my eyes followed by a sharp crack and a roll of thunder. "That was close," I thought.

Getting out of bed and gazing across the lake towards the Butte, I saw a trail of smoke rising off to the left and about half way up the mountain.

Because it was just above town and the Fire Department was down below, my wife and I conversed that it would be put out shortly. However, the smoke thickened and the flames spread. No one seemed to be reacting.

Later, we drove to town to take in the *Art in the Park* displays. Dark billows of smoke could be seen through the trees. The normal crowd of people was not to be seen. Some of the vendors were packing up their displays. We drove home to Chelan Hills and viewed the Butte fire from our deck.

We watched planes with buckets scooping water from the lake to dump on the fire. Bucket after bucket was dumped. All of a sudden a huge DC 10 jet tanker swooped around our place, being led by a small pointer plane. It reminded me of a scared bird being chased by a giant eagle. The small plane was leading the DC 10 to strategic spots to dump a load of red retardant. We watched load after load being dumped. It was quite a show.

Towards the town, huge clouds of black smoke kept rising. Curiosity getting the best of me, I jumped in the truck with my camera and headed to town to investigate. Following the smoke, I drove towards the Senior Center and parked in their lot.

I noticed folks lining the bank overlooking the river. I joined them and started taking pictures of the flames racing toward us. I'm glad the river separated us from the flames but further down flames had

jumped the river and started up the far bank toward homes.
From out of nowhere, it seemed, came this little bird being chased
by the eagle to dump retardant on the flames and the threatened
houses. The owners had a mess to clean up but their homes were
saved.

Chelan Fruit, on the way to Chelan Falls, wasn't so lucky. The
office was untouched but the packing shed was completely
destroyed, as was Chelan Lumber across the street. A few yards
further down a home was burned.

We have friends who live up McNeil Canyon road to the plateau,
left through wheat fields, left again and a few yards down towards the
Columbia River. Somehow the fire jumped the big river, climbed to
their house and destroyed it, leaving their garage untouched.
They've been rebuilding all winter.

Anyway, after watching the flames die down at the river's edge, I
went back to my truck and discovered that, in my haste, I had
locked my keys inside. Inside the Senior Center I found a kind
man who agreed to run me home to get another set.

The wind was from up lake, so the fire approached the Lakeside
area at a slow pace. From our deck we could see that a curvy
firebreak road had been graded up the Butte. The fire was stopped
dead at the road. I was telling my friend, who lives in Lakeside,
about the road. He said, "A grader didn't make the road. It was all
done by hand."

Written by Don Gray

17:38 *East Hugo Rd, outbuildings on fire, three subjects trying to fight fire, not going to evacuate want a fire truck to their location.*

17:40 *Left the Antoine incident to return to Station 17:45 hours.*

17:46 *Apple Acres Rd, three subjects unable to get out.*

17:50 *At Hugo Rd, no one is here to fight fire. Railroad ties on fire.*

17:59 *Antoine Fire, lost containment line between Washington and Antoine Creek. Washington Creek threatened. All resources pulled off the fire due to fire behavior, not safe at this time.*

18:03 *Reassigned to Clifford and Chestnut streets area. Tied in with other units, worked to cool a large pile of brush over the bank on the gorge. Working Clifford St neighborhood, fire came over the Gorge. Crews reported several roof fires that they were chasing and putting out throughout the night in that neighborhood.*

18:11 *Conducted back burn on the east side of Wilmorth around a single structure where fire was rapidly encroaching from the east and south. PUD pole crews were brushing and applying fire retardant to poles. Engines were roadside for structure protection and water sources. Crew was assigned to Columbia View to prevent spread to an unburned structure and reduce embers from burning structures. Crews worked the West side of Wilmorth to divert fire front from reaching homes and heavy equipment parked in a lot mid-point Wilmorth Rd.*

18:15 *Multiple structures on fire, crew enroute. Worked with crews to protect structures along highway; extinguished fire around two residences. One occupant received medical aid for breathing problems due to smoke and heat exposures. Residences had medium fuels within 20ft of structures, large fuel load of firewood and debris stacked along west side of house. Crew used one tank of water to extinguish fire.*

MY DAY AS "MRS. CHIEF"
August 14, 2015

Weather reports were out. We were expected to have thunder and lightning. It had been such a dry and hot summer that the fire danger was extreme. I would say, "It's so dry here, the dirt will burn."

At 5am we woke up to thunder and lightning. My husband jumped in the shower and left for the station. I watched and I heard the noise from the sky. I saw a lightning strike and it looked like it would have hit in the field behind my house. I went to look and saw nothing, so I dismissed it from my thoughts.

The morning went on and the calls started to come across the radio scanner that sits in my living room. My morning started normal, but the day would not end normal at all. I turned the radio up, so I could listen to my husband's day. It was getting busy on the radio, so I turned on my computer. I was listening to KOZI, reading posts on Facebook and listening to calls on the radio. The fires had begun.

I wasn't sure how bad it was, but at this time I knew our Fire Department was going to be working hard. I heard the 2nd alarms go out. The sound of emergency vehicles could be heard. The request for help from neighboring departments went out. Still, I have heard this before. When I discovered that they were asking for help beyond neighboring departments, I knew the fire was getting big. We had 4 fires!

As my morning went on, I decided that I would try to help in the only way that I could think of. I was listening and reading information as it came in. So, I started sharing this on Facebook. I wanted my family and friends to be informed. Most of all anyone in Chelan needed additional information.

Smoke! We could all see the smoke. The fires were so scattered, it didn't matter where you were and you could see smoke. Then I

83

started to see the smoke come up from the hill behind our home, I pointed it out to the neighbors and called the home that sits all by itself halfway up that hill.

By this time, I knew things were getting worse and fast. Next, came the air support. I had heard that the fire was at Chelan Fruit. So the planes and helicopters seemed to be headed in that direction as well as to the top of the Butte. The radio towers are at the top of the Butte, behind our home. If they lost those radio towers, emergency personnel would lose communication.

This is about the time that I started asking myself, "Is this real - is it getting dangerous?" The smoke behind us was increasing. I couldn't call my husband. His time was very valuable right then. But, I did call one of the office staff. She told me that they were working on the fire behind us and it should be okay. Her concern for what was going on in Chelan was apparent to me—I've known her for many years. I wanted someone to tell me that our home was safe. It was crazy to think that anyone could tell me that, but that's what I wanted anyway.

My repetitive routine began. The planes were everywhere. I could watch the helicopters pick up water from the lake, along with the planes dipping to refill. They would fly over our houses, sometimes very close. So I decided that I wanted pictures of the event. I would go outside and take pictures, then return back to my computer and listen to the scanner, listen to KOZI on the radio, as well as reposting on Facebook. I called my mom to let her know what was going on and that I was safe. I didn't want her to see it on the news and worry. I was safe. I did not have fear of the fire. I may be biased, but my husband is well known throughout Washington State with great respect for his knowledge, leadership and experience as a firemen.

As time went on, I decided that I should make a quick trip to the store for a couple of things, so off I went. The store was closed. I could see it from my home. I parked my car and got out to go into the store. It was strange; there were groups of people standing in the parking lot. All of them were looking in the direction of my home. I turned to look and reality hit. That hill behind my home blocked my view of what was going on. That lightning strike that I thought hit the field behind our home, did hit but on the other side of the hill. I could see the fire from the parking lot and it was spreading. It was headed towards our town and my home! I was certainly concerned at this point. So I got what I needed and headed home. Back to my routine, pictures, listening and reposting. Now I started wondering, *Am I going to have to evacuate?*

Hours went by. In the past, I have listened to fire calls and by this time I would have heard something positive about the fire fight. This wasn't happening. They were getting help from around the state and the air support was increasing. I think the planes made me more nervous than the smoke. That DC-10 looked like it was going to scrape its belly on my neighbor's tree.

Evacuation? Do I have to do that? Well maybe. So I started thinking about what I would want. If it was going to happen, then I needed to be ready. I started taking things and piling them up in the middle of my living room. I couldn't put it in a car, still being in denial. So now it was, take pictures, listen, repost on Facebook and gather items for evacuation. Then the doorbell rang. I had 2 fire fighters from Manson at my door. They were going through the area checking homes for defensible space. Our home was looking good, but the home next door was a concern. So I had a possible tinderbox next to my home and I hoped that wouldn't become an issue. Then the Sheriff showed up. I had been placed on Level 2 Evacuation. There it is *Evacuation!* I was fine at the moment, but Level 3 Evacuation is leave and I wasn't there...yet.

Well now, things have changed. Facebook was getting very busy with information and postings. As I tried to keep people informed I had many friends/family that sent messages and would ask questions. I answered as best as I could, but now I had to think about loading up a vehicle. What did I need? What is it that I can't live without? Memories were my highest priority, such as items that I saved when our kids were babies, blankets made by my Grandmother and her Grandmother, my wedding dress, pictures off the wall and 10 huge boxes of pictures that I have yet to scan. Those boxes were all

85

downstairs of course and I took them one at a time to the truck. Then there were our passports, insurance information, medical records and birth certificates. Oh my, those were all in the top 2 drawers of the file cabinet. I wasn't going to go through and search for those, so I took both cabinet drawers! Of course they were downstairs also! I look at those now and I'm amazed I did that. Those were big heavy full metal drawers. I also planned on taking my computer hard drive and back up drive, but I wouldn't do that until the last minute. Then most of all were the items from our loved ones that are no longer with us. That's all we have now, they are gone and I wasn't going to lose that part of them too. I have a shoe in my garden. It has hens and chicks planted in it. That shoe was one of those items. It's the shoe my father wore the day he went to the hospital and never came home again. I cried when I realized that I didn't have room for my Grandmothers treadle sewing machine. I cherish it. I inherited my sewing talents from her.
So my routine had changed somewhat. I had the radio very loud so I could go through the house and gather items. I would go outside, take more pictures and check in with the neighbors. The winds had increased and I knew that was not good. I went back inside to check on Facebook and re-post as I could. By this time, I was feeling emotional. Most of the time, I had tears running down my face. I just ignored it and let it happen. I had things to do. During the day, I would check and see how our neighbors were doing. They were lucky to have their kids there to help, with their evacuation. I was not so lucky, since our kids and family live several hours away. It was hard and scary, facing the fact that I was going to be doing this evacuation alone. Being the Fire Chiefs wife means, I can be alone at a moment's notice. Most times, that's ok, but I was scared. My husband, Tim, was busy, saving lives and property. I hadn't talked to him all day. I did get a few phone calls with messages from him, but I didn't expect him to call unless things were under control and they were not under control.

My new reality was we could lose our home. I knew that homes were being lost near Chelan Fruit and the warehouse was on fire. South Shore was losing homes on the waterfront and homes were threatened just east of me. What most people don't know about my husband is his dedication to his town. He knows that I'm smart enough to stay safe. He would choose to save another's home and sacrifice ours as long as I was safe. So, yes we could lose our home and the flames were coming over the hill. So the truck was packed and I could not get anything else in it. As the fire got closer to the flat area of the field, I decided it was time to go. Bogart, our dog, and I were in the truck. I took one last picture then headed out the driveway. As I left, I then saw that 2 engines, a brush truck and the Sheriff were on our street. I stopped and talked to one Volunteer and left. I was headed to a friend's home on the other side of the lake, but I stopped at the Fire Station first. I hadn't seen my husband all day. It must have been about 4pm. I was hoping to see my husband and get a little support, as well as reassurance that our home would survive. When I arrived at the fire station, I was able to see, the seriousness of this day. I walked into the room where my husband was. There was a group of a dozen or more officials around a table with maps spread out. They were discussing locations of the fires and current situations of each. I stood there for about 10 minutes and even had eye contact once with my husband, but our town's situation was too serious for me to interrupt. Later in the week, I was talking to Tim and mentioned stopping by the Fire Station and he did not recall my being there. He was so focused on his responsibilities to our town that he looked right at me and didn't see me. It was just as well, because I would have melted if he had stopped to reassure me. So I left and went to our friends and we all watched from their deck as they dropped fire retardant on the field behind our home. We could see that the fire was out. I waited for another hour or so and decided to go back home and hoping I still had one. It looked like I did, but I had to see for myself.

At 8pm, I arrived back at our home. It was saved! I could see a line of the fire retardant in the field. We were lucky! Not only had firefighters stopped the fire, but they saved the 2 homes up in the field also. Plus, they didn't have to dump the red stuff on our home. I have heard that it's quite the job to get that off. But, cleaning is better than ashes. Our power was out, but I was happy to have a home. We have a generator, but it wasn't co-operating so candles and flashlights were just fine. I finally saw Tim about 1:30am and he started up the generator, went to sleep for 2 hours then went back to the station. The weeks in front of him would be long and demanding.

My day on August 14, 2015, will never be forgotten. My boxes of pictures will not go downstairs until I get them scanned. Those papers that I should have had together before are now together and accessible. I now have a list of those items that mean so much to us, like my dad's shoe, not to be forgotten. Being prepared is important for everyone, even the Fire Chief's wife.

Written by Cathy Lemon

SPREADING DIRECTIONS

18:29 *South Lake Rd fire is coming towards that area*

18:31 *Bear Mountain has been evacuated.*

18:37 *Antoine Fire, all engine resources off the fire, two dozers with bosses on fire are in the black, can't make it off the fire, will move when the heat cools down.*

18:40 *Level 3 Evacuation for Cagle Gulch and Union Valley.*

18:50 *Apple Acres Rd tied in with USFS crews working structure protection. Additional resources had come off the airfield to assist since air ops were terminated due to darkness. As situation became direr we became more fluid moving up and down SR97/Wilmorth/Columbia View and Apple Acres.*

18:53 *Hydrants are dead in the commercial area.*

19:21 *Chelan Fruit on SR150 has things exploding and fire reached South Lakeshore Road about 100 yards west of the State Park.*

19:31 *PUD trying to force power into Chelan specifically Woodin & Saunders area so we can try to get a few gas stations working.*

19:47 *Residence Wilmorth has a shed on fire, residence is not on fire but it appears as though it will be shortly as well as the residence next door.*

FIRE ON THE MOUNTAIN

Most of us have grown up with Boy Scout and Christmas Eve images of friendly fire; kids circled and singing around summer-camp bonfires and, Santa, resting with milk and cookies within a well-worn, wingback chair and seated before a cheerful blaze contained by a river-stone surround. These images provide comfort and joy. Fire and the heat it creates has provided warmth and security for thousands of years, cooked or burned our steaks on the backyard BBQ and inspired the creation of artificial, electric and DVD replicates for those within apartments and small homes not blessed with a functional fireplace.

We love fire, as long as it stays "put," in the places humanity has designated and within our sense of control. We build facilities to ensure that control. Our common culture glorifies those who help with the control; we love the clanging "fire-red" engines screaming down the street, the fearless heroes on ladders, and the loyal, spotted Dalmatian dogs. For most people, a "burn" happens to a finger when accidentally brushing against a hot stove or handling a heated pot without a protective pad. For most people, a "serious" fire is something that happens to someone else. It may engulf an entire house. At worst, it may destroy an apartment building. But it is always, within hours, contained.

It is not like this for those of us who grew up or still live within the mountains. A cigarette, tossed carelessly from a car. A family campfire hastily and thoughtlessly abandoned, the careless ignition of fireworks in a field, an off-road vehicle bouncing through dehydrated undergrowth, a strike of lightning in the middle of a summer night; all these and more, put the homes and cabins and wildlife of Eastern Washington at the mercy of others and nature, edging our days throughout the "season," with unease and concern as tourists and summer families fill our communities for vacations and holidays. Many of those who have chosen the mountain lifestyle are located at the end of twisted, dirt and gravel roads, many miles away from shiny fire stations and fire hydrants. A few others, like my own family, have situated a few cabins in the northern reaches of Lake Chelan, where there are no roads at all. We made these choices for ourselves, relinquishing the sense of control most have within the cities. No one forced any of us. We chose the lifestyle for the peace and near-silence of the forest. We gave up the security of police and fire sirens for the whisper of wind in the trees, the brush of water on shoreline boulders; for conversations in the summer air instead of television and hand-held devices and for the privilege of catching a glimpse of mule deer and mountain goat on the hills.

In 2001 a blaze, which became known as the Rex Creek Fire, crossed the mountains in a down lake run, and blasted through the small cluster of cabins on the Canoe Creek point. Those of us who were able had made our way up lake to protect the cabins, in private boats against headwinds of nearly 40 mph. The fire had already burned the water lines by the time some of us arrived. Other family members, who had preceded us, spent the night out on the lake in their boat, watching as the fire swept southward on the north shore, seeming to consume everything in its path, including the family cabins.

Through the smoke and haze of early dawn, we gratefully discovered that several buildings remained and spent the next several days hauling water out of the lake by hand. We dragged ourselves up and over the stones of the shore – spilling most of the contents of the buckets in the effort – and dropped the pitiful remnants of lake water at the base of burning trees. We learned, painfully, that searing ash sifts over the tops of shoes and burns the skin inside socks; that spilled water on ash creates a substance more slippery than ice. We learned forested areas, which have experienced any tree cutting or logging, leave stumps which burn downward, into the ground. We learned that these stumps, covered with ash and maintaining coals in the 2000F range, have been known to sear the legs off the unsuspecting and unobservant who step into them; and without protective face and lung protection, our eyes became caked with filth and we would cough black mud from lungs and blow black mucus from noses for weeks. At night, walking along the path between the remaining cabins, the coals of incinerated stumps glowed eerily into the dark; the mountains lit with hundreds of orange and red hot-spots which reminded me of childhood picture books of Christmas elves and gnomes who rested contentedly beneath the earth, before their cheerful and contained hearth fires. My imagination masked the unspoken terror between us.

It was therefore, a clarion call to my family as news spread of numerous fires growing rapidly within the mountain regions of Lake Chelan in this summer of 2015. One of the fires–smoldering outside the tiny mountain community of Holden Village for weeks–had suddenly burst its self-confinement of a few acres, and was now tearing toward and around the village. Our family cabins, although on the opposite side of the lake for this, the Wolverine Fire, were still at risk: winds bearing live embers travel easily for up to five miles. Any tree left dead after the Rex Creek Fire, was now fodder and fuel for any ember, which might travel the quarter mile span from south to north shore in this portion of the lake. Family and friends who had gathered at the cabins for relaxation found themselves relocating woodpiles, raking mounds of pine needles away from buildings and packing their bags in case the worst should happen, again.

As daylight faded from the summer sky, several significant points of firelight emerged on the mountain peaks south of Holden, across the lake. We gathered on the dock, some seated, some holding children, and watched, aghast and helpless as the fire surged and swept across the mountain behind Twin Harbor and toward the populated areas of Chelan. The fire-wind pushed five and six inch embers across the lake and into our hair, our cabins; the wilderness behind us. If it flamed the north shore, we would have to leave.

I watched the fire sweep and engulf the mountains. I imagined the terrified animals which had no recourse, no boat, no way out of the inferno. I watched the tortured trees burst and echo like thunder and bombs. I remembered the sickening damage our own mountain had endured, years earlier. I remembered the unwilling tears streaking down the grime coated face of my cousin as his father and I arrived to help.

This time, I sat, with the others, watching the fire reflect on the blue-black water of the lake. Six sailboats under motor power, with their sails snugged primly to their masts, moved silently, ghostly, northward, toward Prince Creek; their silhouettes dark and quietly defiant against the fire on the mountain. I wondered when our next turn might be. I longed for winter.

Written by Cathy Morehead

19:55 As night fall came, the fire activity began to slow down, but the front was still steadily creeping down the hillside towards homes on West Main Ave. Crews were placed along West Main Ave (across from the Lady of the Lake,) as another unidentified apparatus was up the private drive, just Southwest of West Main Ave. They were prepping two to three homes along the private driveway. The fire was still above those structures. We lined the back yards (thick brush and trees) of the homes on West Main Ave. We supported the burnout physically by not letting the homes on West Main Ave. burn. Within minutes the three structures on the private drive went up in flames as we continued to wet the houses and vegetation below due to falling embers.

20:18 New Mexico Type-6 Strike Team had just arrived.

20:23 Fire is moving down the slope toward town from Chelan Falls

20:24 Fire was starting to consume heavy fuels around Hatchery and had burned 10x20 foot storage building to the north of Hatchery

21:07 Chelan Falls, vehicle broken down in his driveway, needs a ride out, two people and a dog.

21:11 Need law enforcement on Wilmorth Drive, Firefighter in an assault situation. Crew working on a better location, it's in progress. On Wilmorth just north of Isenhart, request ETA from law enforcement.

Firefighters reported an agitated civilian was complicating operations. Seemed to be resolved for the moment but the civilian reappeared, took a poke at one of the firefighters. Requested Law Enforcement and they arrived and handled the situation.

Unappraised Value

We can inventory things that are lost, scrapbook family photos, look through granddad's old slides for documentation. But there is little insurance because true value does not reside in things with a price tag. It comes from our labor, fellowship, family, vacations and refuge, matchmaking and weddings on the dock, rain on the cabin roof.

We built it ourselves over fifty years—one nail at a time with recycled material. No receipts. No value to the County Assessor.

How do you perform an appraisal on love?

So now we will build again, over the next fifty years, new generations mixing the cement this time. No status symbols or amenities of glass and chrome with flushable toilets. But we will have pride of workmanship, the feel of concrete and wood in our hands, generations coming together to create a place of love, laughter, music and sharing. Love of place, history and tradition, stories, and memories of a lifetime...these are the real valuables.

You can't insure them.
You can't assess them.

Because you cannot inventory sweat, love, memories or tradition, you can only honor them as you haul your buckets of sand down the steep hill with a smile on your face and joy in your heart. The cabins are gone, but the moon still rises over the silvery lake, the osprey family will find a new tree, new growth will appear and the love is always here.

An old metal doorknob
retrieved from mountains of ash
my only souvenir

Written by Nancy Culp

95

Area Estimated Business Loss of Revenue

Infrastructure, tenant dwellings, product damage, closed doors and numerous issues caused income loss.

0-$2,5000	6.10%
$2,501-5,000	9.76%
$5,001-10,000	23.17%
$10,001-25,000	24.39%
$25,001-50,000	10.98%
$50,001-100,000	8.54%
$100,000+	17.07%
	82 Responses

Proprietor Concerns for Employees

*Loss of Employee Income and/or Benefits**

Inability to gain immediate Employment	33.33%
Eligibility for Unemployment Benefits	8.89%
Funds for Employee Salaries during Business Re-development	75.56%
	45 Responses

*Employees were laid off or lost their jobs. Construction halted. All annual events cancelled. City income dwindled.

Employees suffered from poor air quality and psychological stress.

Chelan Fires of August 14-28, 2015

A resounding crack of thunder made me bolt out of bed around 5:30a.m. Friday August 14th. I immediately looked out my bedroom window toward the Butte and saw where lightning had left a circular burned patch in the grass. There were no flames at first, but in a short while flames could be seen moving slowly out of the circle. A short-lived rain seemed to douse the flames, but they reappeared and began creeping out making a larger area of fire. There were several more thunder and lightning events, but none that I could see caused more fire starts on the Butte.

I kept looking out the window toward the Butte expecting to see a fire truck and crew get to the fire, but that didn't happen. Surely people in the neighborhood would be getting up to the fire with shovels and wet gunny sacks to put the fire out, but that didn't happen either. The fire was spreading more and more, heading up the Butte toward the towers and west toward places where there were houses and orchards. It was a couple hours before I saw a truck arrive below the fire, but firemen didn't walk toward the fire right away.

We remembered hearing in the past that only fire fighters from the group that manages a fire area, such as Fish and Wild Life, BLM, and the Nat'l Forest Service, can respond to a fire in their jurisdiction. This has led to incredibly long responses to local fires in the past years. More recent information was given to say the Chelan Fire Department can respond to any fire in the area until the "official designated" group can get there. So where was our fire department, and why the long response time until a crew was activated on the fire?

It was several hours before we saw helicopters dropping water on the largely expanded Butte fire. In time, a spotter plane directed a DC-10 bomber with borate fire retardant to fly low over the flames that were reaching homes. As the retardant loads were depleted, the plane would fly back to Moses Lake for refills. Other loud, powerful bombers carrying massive amounts of water would drop their loads, turn back to the lake near Campbell's, and swoop directly down over the bridge and graze the lake to scoop up water for another run. People on the bridge, watching and taking photos, were mesmerized by these spectacular maneuvers!

Our friends, Kathy and Larry, live along First Creek Rd. which was already in a major fire area. They had brought their computers, valuables, and important papers to our basement area for storage on Thursday. On Friday, they came to stay at the house after receiving a Level 3 Evacuation notice to leave their property. There was quite a collection of personal and pet gear as they arrived with their suitcases, and cages with two dogs and three birds, and carriers for three cats with food and bowls for each one. The downstairs kitchen floor and kitchen table filled up quickly.

After they settled in, we were conversing when someone knocked on the door. I opened it to my friend, Patty, who asked if she and Nels could come in because they had just lost their house and everything in it. She had managed to leave in her car with papers, jewelry, and a few changes of clothes; sadly, she couldn't get her cat in its carrier so it was left in the house. Nels came in his pickup with their big Airedale and a bag of dog food but no other personal belongings. As they left their property, she said there were fire trucks above their driveway so they asked the fire fighters to go down to their property, but the response was "we don't have the authority to go there." (During this event we learned that complex fires are managed by the Incident Command Service that coordinates the different agencies so everyone knows where each one is and what they are doing. Crews cannot divert from their assignments.)

Patty and Nels with Cody dog got settled in an upstairs bedroom and she began making calls to their family. Her cell phone wasn't working well so she used mine. Tooth brushes, toothpaste, and other essentials were given to them. Nels retired in the bedroom to contemplate all they had lost and what they would be facing.

As we continued through the afternoon, we were rather subdued as we saw the whole Butte blackened with wind-whipped fires traveling in every direction up to the towers, further west into the neighborhoods around the high school, and on down into the gorge area. More evacuations were taking place on the hills all the way to Slide Waters. Radio reports gave information about other lightning strike fires all around the Chelan area. We busied ourselves with dinner preps and as the evening darkness came, we were astounded when we looked out and saw what appeared to be hundreds of campfires in flame over the entire Butte.

The next day, we knew that the First Creek Fire had worsened, threatening Watson's Resort and lakeside residences. The Wolverine Fire was threatening Holden Village and heading down lake toward 25 Mile Creek. As the day went on reports came in that the Chelan Fresh packing sheds, the Chelan Building Supply, and a new winery had burned, plus several homes along the Wilmorth Rd. area. The fire had gone down toward the powerhouse at Chelan Falls, up Deer Mountain on over toward the Rodeo Grounds, and down to Howard Flats and Apple Acres. It even jumped the Columbia River to go into McNeil Canyon. Fire along Antoine Creek had taken out homes and was threatening to spread south to Union Valley and Purtteman Gulch.

Each day we would scan signboards around town posted with updated information on the fires, complete with maps and reports of firefighting being done in each fire area. It would be days before the community would know the total widespread destruction of homes, businesses, and property that devastated the valley.

On Tuesday following the initial Butte event, power was lost to KOZI, regular and cell phone service, TVs, and computers. Several days without communication created an eerie realization of how much we depend on these services. We lighted several candles and found flashlights and a battery operated radio. We remembered not to open refrigerator and freezer doors so foods would stay cold and be slow to thaw. Fortunately, having a gas stove top and the BBQ allowed meat and perishables to be cooked as they thawed so food loss was minimal. As several cartons of ice cream melted, I offered them with straws to everyone.

A humorous incident came about when Richard decided we needed fried potatoes with the steaks he'd be BBQing, but there were no potatoes in the house so he and Larry went to the store. Without power, there were no lights and shoppers were roaming around dark aisles looking for items with the light from their cell phones. Cash registers were not working so sales were cash or check. No power at the clinics; doctors were hand-writing prescriptions on paper to be carried to the pharmacies. Downtown streets were empty because stores and service stations were closed. Intense smoke and lack of conveniences at stores, restaurants, and hotels were causing tourists to leave town. This was initially prevented when roads into and out of Chelan were closed to allow fire equipment and crews to come into the area. Local people who had been out of town couldn't enter town to get back to their homes.

The Wenatchee PUD brought a large generator to KOZI to restore radio broadcasting. A natural gas truck was driven up to the towers on the Butte to replenish the empty tank with propane that is needed to power cell phone senders and receivers. Long, hard hours of work by crews from the PUD and phone companies got those systems back on line to most areas in a few days and people were relieved to have communication restored.

Patty and Nels moved in with their neighbors to be closer to their destroyed property. Kathy and Larry and their menagerie were with us for a week. As the First Creek Fire became less threatening to their area, they were allowed onto their property for short periods to assess damage. A storage shed, with boat and outdoor equipment, had burned down and their irrigation system had a couple melted pipes that needed to be replaced so water could be turned back onto their acreage.

Firefighter camps set up at Chelan Falls and Beebe Park housed 1000 fire fighters and the National Guard who were in the valley, many from other counties and states. They would be here for weeks. Huge out of control fires were now roaring through Douglas and Okanogan Counties requiring even more fire fighters. Sadly, three young men were killed and another burned severely when the truck they were driving out of a fire was overtaking by flames.

After the road along South Shore was opened to general traffic, we drove to 25 Mile Creek, astounded by the burned areas right down to the road that had taken out a dozen homes near Watson's Resort. Fire had burned hot and black to the tops of ridges and hot spots were still visible. After the 2014 Carlton Complex fire, we had driven up Indian Dan Canyon Road through the burned areas clear to Loup Loup. Trees in those fires had burned so hot that they were the blackest black we'd ever seen and they stood like specters. The bare ground looked sterile from the intense heat. I was expecting trees in the burned forests above South Shore to look the same. However, it was incredible that there were still areas of unburned growth next to and inside burned areas with dried trees and brush that could instantly be another fire if hit by lightning. We realized the local forests are still vulnerable for more fires at any time.

The Chelan Complex Fire event was unique and unforgettable. Hearing that more friends lost homes and property was extremely sad. People were eager to help in any way possible, and the Red Cross and our own Valley Hope were busily taking care of immediate needs. The days continued to be different and out-of-sync, leaving us emotionally torn and feeling fragmented as we waited for a sense of normalcy to return.

Written by Susan McKinnon

0900 *Aug 24, 2015 Weather: Red Flag conditions continue through 9:00 pm on Tuesday including continued moderate instability creating critical fire weather conditions today. Temperatures: upper 80s to lower 90s, mid to upper 70s on the ridges. Relative humidity: 14-19%. Light west/northwest winds 2-4 mph are expected in the AM, becoming 10-15 mph in afternoon, gusts up to 20 mph.*

0900 *Aug 24, 2015, Chelan Complex/Wolverine/First Creek Fires Update: Yesterday crews made good progress strengthening containment lines along the southern and eastern portion of the fire. Fireline along Cooper Ridge on the western edge is holding well. Today crews continue strengthening line for firing operations in unburnt fuel pockets to reduce fuel loads where access allows. Firefighters will patrol containment lines, monitor for spot fires, and extinguish flare-ups in areas of unburned fuels insides the fire perimeter. Dozer line will continue to be constructed along the Forest Service 600 Road near South Fork Gold Creek. Portions of the Chelan Complex within three miles of Chelan and all areas east of the Columbia River are completely contained*

0900 *Aug. 28th, 2015 Weather: Weather will be changing throughout the day. In the morning, winds will be light and variable with cloud cover providing stability. The Wolverine fire may experience light rain in the morning to afternoon, with a 20% chance of wetting rain. Humidity in this area is expected to rise up to 35%. The Chelan Complex fire will experience comparatively drier weather, with wetting rain unlikely and humidity topping out at about 32%. Wind is expected to increase in the afternoon to evening with gusts up to 20 mph and humidity rising up to 60%. A strong cold front is expected to move through the area Friday night into Saturday, bringing with it high winds and potential for heavy rain in the Wolverine fire area.*

0900 *Aug. 28th, 2015 Chelan Complex/Wolverine/First Creek Fires Update: Chelan Complex: Yesterday, the fire crossed the line at South Fork Gold Creek on the north side. Crews are scouting opportunities to construct a dozer line. Goat Mountain continues to be closely monitored. Crews will continue to patrol and mop up the fire along the western flank today. Due to minimal fire activity, the southern portion of the fire will be monitored by air today.*

1700 to 0900 *Aug. 28-29, 2015 Strike Team Leader, Brush 73, 75, Engine 79, Tender 74, 75 with a total of 11 personnel worked the South Lakeshore Fire nightshift.*

STATS

Chelan County Assessor Destroyed Property Report:
<u>Damaged and/or Lost</u> - 30 Residential/Commercial and 28 Outbuildings

NW Interagency Coordination Center's Report dated (09/08/2015):
<u>Destroyed</u> - 21 Residences and 23 minor structures
<u>Threatened</u> - 150 Commercial property and 650 minor structures
<u>Total of 800</u> structures threatened/saved, content not included

Residential/Commercial	Outbuildings	Total Value	Location
25 - $23,320,263	19 - $39,725	$23,359,988	Chelan
4 - 116,876	7 - 36,502	153,378	Antoine/WA Creek
1 - No Value Assigned	2 - No Value	$0	Union Valley
30 - $23,437,139	28 - $76,227	$23,513,366	Totals

FEMA was unable to assist financially due to Eastern Washington's rural, widespread demographics. A Representative was sent to Washington D.C. to address changing this verbiage and to discuss restructuring policies regarding firefighting jurisdictions.

Meanwhile, post-fire networking, area counseling and local financial donations were provided.

We truly live in a giving, compassionate community!